The
COUNTRY HOUSE
COMPANION

Published
by
Moonrise Press, Ludlow 2011

ISBN 978–0–9539561–9–7

Printed in Great Britain

The COUNTRY HOUSE COMPANION

DAVID PHILLIPS

MOONRISE PRESS

CONTENTS

PREFACE

There are many good books about country houses: detailed guidebooks to individual properties, and general ones on particular themes, styles, or periods. I wrote this book because I needed something different. As I admire, say, a Humphrey Repton landscape, I like to check up what he was famous for, where else he worked, and when. The distinction between Baroque and Late Baroque sometimes slips my mind. And did I ever know the difference between a calash and a carriole? In short, I needed a reference book I could take with me on visits, containing enough information to enhance my visit, without requiring a footman to carry it. Come to think of it, *was* that a footman's job? If you ever ask yourself this sort of question, this book is for you. It aims to provide in a concise fashion a working knowledge of the country house and of those who built, furnished and landscaped such houses, as well as something of the lifestyles of their inhabitants.

Nobody knows for sure how many country houses there are in the United Kingdom. Some are privately owned, but many have become schools, colleges, or hotels. The National Trust (which covers England, Wales and Northern Ireland) and The National Trust for Scotland own over 200 houses, the Landmark Trust about 75, and English Heritage about 50. Some 600 are open to the public for all or part of the time.

There are many definitions of a country house, but here it means a large non-fortified house in the country, surrounded by gardens and an estate that supported it, or still do. Castles and ecclesiastical buildings that have become country houses are included, but ruins are not.

The scene is set by an explanation of the major styles and periods in which country houses were built, followed by brief details of the lives of the major architects, landscape architects and craftsmen who worked on them. At the end of each entry there is a list of the most important country houses (and occasionally some other buildings) that were designed, extended or landscaped by the person described, or where their work may be seen today.

There are sections on construction, rooms and their purposes, furnishings and contents, and on gardens and estate buildings.

Finally the country house lifestyle is addressed: servants, meals, horse drawn carriages, musical instruments, the Season, dancing and other pastimes. The book concludes with a list—perhaps a little bit sad to many—of all the country houses mentioned, saying, as far as one can tell, what has become of them now.

David Phillips
March 2011

ENGLISH AND WELSH COUNTY ABBREVIATIONS AS USED IN THIS BOOK

Beds	Bedfordshire	Leics	Leicestershire
Berks	Berkshire	Lincs	Lincolnshire
Bristol	Bristol	London	Greater London
Bucks	Buckinghamshire	Norfolk	Norfolk
Cambs	Cambridgeshire	Northants	Northamptonshire
Carms	Carmarthanshire	Northumb	Northumberland
Ches	Cheshire	Notts	Nottinghamshire
Conwy	Conwy	Oxon	Oxfordshire
Cornwall	Cornwall	Pembs	Pembrokeshire
Cumb	Cumbria	Powys	Powys
Den	Denbighshire	Rut	Rutland
Derbys	Derbyshire	Salop	Shropshire
Devon	Devonshire	Som	Somerset
Dorset	Dorset	Staffs	Staffordshire
Durham	County Durham	Suffolk	Suffolk
Essex	Essex	Surrey	Surrey
Flints	Flintshire	Sussex	Sussex
Glam	Glamorganshire*	Tyne & W.	Tyne & Wear
Glos	Gloucestershire	Warwicks	Warwickshire
Gwynedd	Gwynedd	W. Mid	West Midlands
Hants	Hampshire	Wilts	Wiltshire
Herefs	Herefordshire	Worcs	Worcestershire
Herts	Hertfordshire	Yorks (E, N, S, W,)	Yorkshire
IoW	Isle of Wight		
Kent	Kent		
Lancs	Lancashire		

*Includes the present counties of Blaenau Gwent, Bridgend, Caerphilly, Cardiff, Merthyr Tydfil, Neath Port Talbot, Newport, Rhondda Cynon Taff, Swansea, Torfaen and Vale of Glamorgan.

THE HISTORICAL VALUES OF £1 STERLING

YEAR	VALUE OF £1	YEAR	VALUE OF £1
1300	£10,400	1650	£1,590
1325	£8,150	1675	£1,500
1350	£7,420	1700	£1,660
1375	£5,250	1725	£1,630
1400	£5,480	1750	£1,500
1425	£5,140	1775	£1,360
1450	£5,440	1800	£798
1475	£4,930	1825	£805
1500	£4,930	1850	£774
1525	£4,930	1875	£521
1550	£3,920	1900	£436
1575	£2,530	1925	£189
1600	£2,020	1950	£76
1625	£1,840	1975	£10

The table above gives the approximate purchasing power of £1 for every twenty-five years since 1300. So, for example, to calculate the value of £50 in 1500, multiply £4,930 by 50, which gives £246,250. The calculations are taken from www.measuringworth.com, which points out that there are many ways of calculating relative values, and that in every case calculations are bound to be approximate. In this table, the 'Average Earnings' comparator was chosen as being the most useful. These are the values used throughout this book to compute costs at present-day prices.

STYLES AND PERIODS

Historical styles are described in several ways. The reigns of monarchs or dynasties may be used to indicate either a date range or a style or both (e.g. Jacobean, Queen Anne, Georgian). Architectural terms are also employed (baroque, rococo), as are the names of originators of styles (Adam, Palladian), of movements (Arts and Crafts, Art Nouveau), and descriptive terms (Chinoiserie, Picturesque). Many styles regained their popularity at a later date. For example, Palladian had two revivals, and Jacobean, Queen Anne and many more came into vogue in the late Victorian period. The nomenclature of such styles will often reflect this (Gothic Revival/Neo-Gothic, Renaissance Revival etc.).

ADAM STYLE (1760–90). A Neo-classical style that emphasized symmetry and order in a reaction against the exuberance of the Baroque. Distinguished by graceful lines and slender ornamentation with light mouldings. Originated by Robert Adam and his brother, James.

ART NOUVEAU (1880–1910). A decorative style, mainly applied to furniture and interior decoration, which spread under different names from England to Europe and America. Art Nouveau was an innovative style, contrasting with the imitation ones that characterized most of the Victorian period. Charles Rennie Mackintosh was its chief exponent among British architects.

ARTS AND CRAFTS (1860–1920). A social and aesthetic movement that emerged in England in the mid-nineteenth century in reaction to the mechanisation of the Victorian era. It promoted good design, using simple shapes, and craftsmanship, and embraced printing, wallpaper-making, furniture and many other crafts as well as architecture. John Ruskin, A. W. N. Pugin, William Morris, Norman Shaw, Philip Webb and Charles Voysey were the foremost exponents of this style.

BAROQUE (1660–1730). A theatrical, not to say ostentatious, style which originated in Rome in the late sixteenth century and spread throughout Europe. It was brought to England at the Restoration. Its significant features were massiveness, emphatic overstatement and vigorous ornamentation. In England, the principal architects were Sir

DATE	PERIOD	MAIN STYLES
1450	Late Mediaeval	Late Gothic
1500	Tudor	Renaissance Tudor Elizabethan Jacobean
1550	Elizabethan	
1600	Jacobean	
1650	Commonwealth	Baroque William and Mary Queen Anne
	Restoration	
1700	William and Mary	
	Queen Anne	
1750	Georgian	Palladian Rococo (Late Baroque) Neo-classical Adam Picturesque
1800	Regency	Italianate Greek Revival Gothic Revival/Neo-Gothic Chinoiserie
1850	Victorian	Tudorbethan Jacobethan Renaissance Revival Arts & Crafts
1900	Edwardian	Art Nouveau Queen Anne Style

John Vanbrugh and Nicholas Hawksmoor, and in furniture design it was characterized by heavy decoration, and exuberant and irregular surfaces and curves.

CHINOISERIE, CHINESE (1750–1800). A derivative style of Rococo. Fanciful, exotic motifs derived from Chinese originals were applied to European architecture, furniture and interior design. Elaborately painted lacquer is a common feature of Chinoiserie furniture.

ELIZABETHAN (1550–1600). Characterized by an H– or E–shaped plan, a mixture of Gothic (large mullioned and transomed windows) and Renaissance elements (columns), extravagant rooflines (chimneys, turrets), enthusiastic and sometimes grotesque decoration (strapwork, obelisks) and general ebullience (chimney pieces). Particularly large, magnificent late Elizabethan or Jacobean houses (1550–1630) are known as 'Prodigy buildings' or 'Prodigy houses'.

GOTHIC REVIVAL (1750–1900). This revival began as a romantic admiration of the Gothic style. Gradually in the course of the nineteenth century it developed into an almost religious revival, opposing the 'pagan' Renaissance styles and dominating the century.

GREEK REVIVAL (1780–1840). See also NEO-CLASSICAL. A style based on a accurate study of Greek buildings, springing from James ('Athenian') Stuart's (1713–88) and Nicholas Revett's (1720–1804) visits to Greece and Stuart's *Antiquities of Athens* (published in five volumes between 1795 and 1830).

ITALIANATE (1800–60). A style modelled on a type of sixteenth century Italian palazzo. It was thoroughly asymmetrical and characterized by low roofs with deep overhanging eaves, towers and arcades.

JACOBEAN (1600–50). A continuation of the Elizabethan style, which lasted through the reigns of James I (1603–25) and Charles I (1625–49).

JACOBETHAN (1835–85). Nineteenth century revivalist style, mixing Elizabethan and Jacobean styles. See also TUDORBETHAN.

LATE BAROQUE. See ROCOCO.

MEDIAEVAL. Generally, the style of architecture from about the tenth century to the first half of the sixteenth. It includes, therefore, the first century or so of the country house, and is characterized by pointed arches, pointed ribbed vaults, buttresses, spires, window tracery.

NEO-CLASSICAL (1750–1800). A revival of interest in ancient Greek and Roman themes which occurred in England during the late eighteenth century, inspired by archaeological discoveries.

NEO-GOTHIC. See GOTHIC REVIVAL.

PALLADIAN (1720–50). A plain, almost austere, style of classical architecture derived from the work of Andrea Palladio (1508–80) in Veneto and introduced into England by Inigo Jones (1573–1652), who had visited Italy (The Queen's House (1616–35) and the Banqueting House (1619–22), both London). Jones had no successors, and it was not until the early eighteenth century that Palladianism underwent its second revival under Lord Burlington and Colen Campbell. This was much more successful, and from c.1720–50 most new country houses were designed in this style.

PICTURESQUE (1790–1810). Originally a term applied to eighteenth century landscape, derived from the paintings of Lorraine, Rosa and Poussin, and by extension to architecture. 'Natural', following 'Capability' Brown's landscapes, and full of detail and variety. In architecture, it was defined by a lack of symmetry, irregularity, and smallness, as exemplified by the villas of John Nash.

QUEEN ANNE (1702–14) and her immediate predecessors **WILLIAM AND MARY** (1689–1702 and 1689–94). This was the culmination of the Baroque style in major stately homes and the era of Sir John Vanbrugh, Nicholas Hawksmore and Christopher Wren. In country houses some continental influences, mainly from the Netherlands, were seen, such as red brick facings, tall sash windows, and roofs hidden by parapets.

QUEEN ANNE STYLE (1860–1900). A nineteenth century architectural revivalist style. The revival is usually credited to W. E. Nesfield.

RENAISSANCE (fourteenth to sixteenth centuries). This great, Europe-wide rediscovery of classical art and letters began in Italy in the fourteenth century and continued for at least two centuries. In Britain, Renaissance architecture primarily meant the promiscuous application of classical elements until Inigo Jones (1573–1652) based his buildings on Italian models.

ROCOCO (1740–50). A later version of the Baroque and thus also known as Late Baroque. It originated in France and became especially popular in southern Germany and Austria. It was characterized by heavy ornamentation and exuberant and irregular surfaces and curves. It was not common in the UK, but is thought to have influenced Art Nouveau.

TUDOR (1485–1558). An architectural style characterized by diaper brickwork, large mullioned and transomed windows, four-centred arches and elaborate chimneys. Many of these features continued into the Elizabethan and Jacobean styles.

TUDORBETHAN (1870–1900). A nineteenth century revivalist style which mixed Tudor, Elizabethan and Jacobean elements. See also **JACOBETHAN**.

WILLIAM AND MARY. See **QUEEN ANNE**.

COUNTRY HOUSE ARCHITECTS, LANDSCAPE ARCHITECTS AND CRAFTSMEN

The architect, in the sense of one who designs buildings, did not exist in the United Kingdom until the seventeenth century. Before that, country houses were designed and built by master masons or master carpenters, few of whose names are known (Robert Liminge and the Smythsons being exceptions). The architectural profession emerged in Italy in the sixteenth century, spread to France and then England, where the first true architects may be said to have been Inigo Jones and John Thorpe. They were rapidly followed by 'gentlemen' architects such as William Winde, Sir Roger Pratt, and their followers. Architecture as a professional pursuit followed; Sir Robert Taylor was probably the first architect to take apprentices. An apprenticeship in the mid-eighteenth century lasted for five or six years, after which the budding architect would travel to Italy, Sicily, Greece, or Asia Minor, before returning home to seek commissions. In this period, before the spread of architectural patronage, the Office of His Majesty's Works played a major role in granting commissions and getting young architects started.

There were many attempts to organize architecture on the model of other professions, starting with the Royal Society of Arts in 1754, and many clubs and societies existed before the Institute of British Architects received its royal charter in 1837. The spread of the railways from 1840 onwards set the seal on the architectural profession by allowing architects to cover immense distances and spread thier influence far and wide.

Landscape architecture followed a parallel course. The first landscape gardeners whose names we know were the Tradescants (beginning in the late sixteenth century), followed by William Winde and Henry Wise. But gardens evolve, inevitably, and fashions change, and there are therefore few gardens today which survive as their creators planned them: most 'old' gardens are nineteenth and twentieth century reconstructions. But a few do: there are gardens, or parts of gardens, designed by Charles Bridgeman, William Kent, 'Capability' Brown, Humphrey Repton, W. A. Nesfield and Gertude Jekyll.

The case with craftsmen is somewhat different. The names, if not the biographies, of carpenters, masons, plasterers and stuccoists, cabinet makers, decorative painters and clockmakers are reasonably well known from the mid-sixteenth until the early nineteenth centuries, when different forms of mass production and machine manufacture gradually came to hold sway. Even stone could be 'manufactured'— see the career of Eleanor Coade. The Arts and Crafts movement (1860–1920) made a fighting retreat, but the day of the craftsmen as a dominant force was over.

———————————

Where relevant, at the end of each entry there is a list of those country houses and other buildings that were designed, built, worked upon, or supplied by the person described or, in the case of furniture makers and such like, where their work may be seen today.

ADAM, ROBERT (1728–92). Architect, decorator and interior designer. Architect of the King's Works, 1761–9 (with Sir William Chambers). Director of the family firm, assisted by his brothers John (1721–92), James (1732–94) and William (1738–1822). Settled in London in 1758 after completing the Grand Tour. Evolved a characteristic Neo-classical style, the 'Adam style', advocating an integrated design for architecture, interiors and furniture, as illustrated in *The Works in Architecture of Robert and James Adam* (1773–8, 1779).

Dumfries House, Ayrshire (1754–9, with John); Kedleston Hall, Derbys (c.1760–70); Syon House, London (1762–8); Osterley Park, London (1763–80); Nostell Priory, W. Yorks (1765–75, alterations and interiors); Kenwood House, London (1767–9, then in the country); Newby Hall, N. Yorks (1767–74, alterations); Mellerstain House, Borders (c.1770–8, with James); Wedderburn Castle, Borders (1771–5, begun by his father, William); Letterfourie House, Moray (1773); Caldwell House, Ayrshire (1773–4, partly destroyed by fire); St Edmund's Hill, Suffolk (1773–6); Culzean Castle, Ayrshire (1777–92); Brasted Place, Kent (1784–5); Airthrey Castle, Stirling (1790–1); and Stobs Castle, Borders (1792–4).

ADAM, WILLIAM (1689–1748). Architect, landscape architect, building contractor and entrepreneur. Father of John, Robert, James and William. Influenced by James Gibbs and Sir John Vanbrugh.

Lawers House, Perth and Kinross (1724–6, 1737–44); Dalmahoy House (formerly Belverdere), Midlothian (1725–8); The Drum, Midlothian (1726–

30); Arniston House, Midlothian (1726–32); Cumbernauld House, Dunbartonshire (1731); Chatelherault, Lanarkshire (1731–45); Haddo House, Aberdeenshire (1732–5); Duff House, Moray (1735–41); Murdoustoun Castle, Lanarkshire (c 1735–40).

ALBORN, THOMAS (*fl.* 1667–78). Plasterer. Lived in Glasgow. All his recorded work is in Scotland.

Thirlestane Castle, Borders (1671–4); Kinross House, Perth and Kinross (1673); Stirling Palace and Castle, Stirling (1675–6); Hamilton Palace, Lanarkshire (1675–7); and Craighall Castle, Perth and Kinross (1699).

ARCHER, THOMAS (c.1668–1743). Amateur Baroque architect.

North front of Chatsworth House, Derbys (1704–5); Heythrop Park, Oxon (c.1705–8); Chettle House, Dorset (c.1715–20); garden pavilion at Wrest Park, Beds (1709–11); Roehampton House, Surrey (1710–12); and several churches.

ARTARI, GIUSEPPE (?–1769). Stuccoist. Born in Italy. Trained in Rome, Germany, and Holland before coming to England. Often worked with Bagutti or Vassalli.

Duncombe Park, N. Yorks (c.1715, with Vassalli); Octagon House, London (1720, with Bagutti); Ditchley Park, Oxon (1725, with Vassalli); Houghton Hall, Norfolk (1726); Moulsham Hall, Essex (1730–1); Moor Park, Herts (c.1732, with Bagutti); Trentham Hall, Staffs (1737–8); Wimpole Hall, Cambs, (1743–4); Ragley Hall, Warwicks (1756–60). Also the Senate House, Cambridge (1722–30), St Martin-in-the-Fields, London (1722–6), and the Radcliffe Camera, Oxford (1744–5).

BAGUTTI, GIOVANNI, (1681–after 1730). Stuccoist. The senior partner to Artari and, according to Daniel Defoe, 'the finest artist in those particular works now in England'.

Castle Howard, N. Yorks (1710); Cannons, London (before 1720, destroyed 1747); Octagon House, London (1720, with Artari); Mereworth Castle, Kent (1722–5); Moulsham Hall, Essex (1730–1, assisted by Artari); Moor Park, Herts (c.1732, with Artari); and Cassiobury Park, Herts (date uncertain, demolished 1927). Also the Senate House, Cambridge (1722–30) and St Martin-in-the-Fields, London (1722–6).

BARNSLEY, ERNEST (1863–1926) and **SIDNEY** (1865–1926). Arts and Crafts designers and workmen. The brothers were articled as architects, but in 1893 they moved to the Cotswolds, and in 1903 to Sapperton, Glos ('the Sapperton group'). Sidney Barnsley concentrated on furniture-making and became the best of the Cotswold School of furniture makers. The work of the two Barnsleys, much of it in unstained oak, is best studied at Rodmarton Manor, Glos (designed by Ernest Barnsley, 1909).

BARRY, SIR CHARLES (1795–1860). Neo-classical architect, although sometimes in Neo-Gothic clothing, and landscape architect. Mainly public buildings in London: Travellers Club (1829–32), which introduced the Renaissance Revival; Palace of Westminster (1835–60); and Reform Club (1838–41).

> Highclere Castle, Hants (1842–c.1850), and Harewood House, W. Yorks (1844). Rebuilt Cliveden House, Bucks (1850–1) after its destruction by fire. Laid out the gardens at Trentham Hall, Staffs and also remodelled the hall itself (1834–40 and 1840–9, since demolished). Alterations to Kingston Lacy, Dorset (1835–41). Laid out gardens at Shrubland Park, Suffolk (1849–54).

BERNASCONI, FRANCIS (1762–1841). Plasterer.

> Cobham Hall, Kent (1800–9); Shugborough Hall, Staffs (1803, 1805); Windsor Castle, Berks (1805); Compton Place, Sussex (1806); Dodington Park, Glos (1810); Longleat House, Wilts (c.1810); Badminton House, Glos (1811); Eaton Hall, Ches (1812); Ashridge House, Herts (1813–5); Ashburnham Place, Sussex (1813–19); Eastnor Castle, Herefs (1816); Chatsworth House, Derbys (1820–c.1830); and Lilleshall Hall, Staffs (c.1824).

BLOCKLEY, THOMAS (1705–89). Locksmith from Bull Street, Birmingham.

> Supplied goods to: Kirtlington Park, Oxon (1746); Croome Court, Worcs (1760); Holkham Hall, Norfolk (1761); Shardeloes, Bucks (1763); and Harewood House, W. Yorks (1773).

BRIDGEMAN, CHARLES (1690–1738). Royal Gardener, 1728–38. Pioneer of naturalism and pupil of Henry Wise, although his reputation has been overshadowed by those of William Kent and 'Capability' Brown.

> Worked with Sir John Vanbrugh at Blenheim Palace, Oxon (c.1709), and Grimsthorpe Castle, Lincs (about 1715). Had a major hand in the gardens at: Stowe House, Bucks (c.1714); Wimpole Hall, Cambs (c.1720), where the drive is three miles long and 500 feet wide; Claremont House, Surrey (1720s), where he laid out the amphitheatre; Rousham House, Oxon (1720s, Bridgeman's designs completed about 1737); and Houghton Hall, Norfolk (1722–35), where he is said to have invented the ha-ha.

BROMWICH, THOMAS (*fl.* 1740–87). Paper-stainer and paper-hanger (also linen-draper and upholsterer). From London.

Alscot Park, Warwicks (1765); Corsham Court, Wilts (1773); and Croome Court, Worcs (1781).

BROWN, LANCELOT 'CAPABILITY' (1716–83). Landscape architect and architect. Made his name as head gardener at Stowe House, Bucks, where he 'naturalised' the park (1741) with artificial lakes, 'random' clumps of trees and irregular lawns. In 1749 he set up on his own and over the next thirty years created many parks.

Picturesque parks at: Blenheim Palace (1760s), where he naturalised Henry Wise's designs; Berrington Hall, Herefs (1780s); Croome Court, Worcs (1751–2); Bowood House, Wilts (1760s); and Nuneham Park, Oxon (1778–82). His buildings include Croome Court, Worcs, the bridge and chapel at Compton Verney, Warwicks (1770–8) and Claremont House, Surrey (1771–4), Trentham Park (House enlarged wi- Henry Holland 1768-78, Pendroque + Pakh Henry Holland)

BRUCE, SIR WILLIAM (c.1630–1710). Architect. Founder of Classical architecture in Scotland, supporter of the restoration of Charles II, and, under William and Mary, suspected Jacobite.

Altered and enlarged: Brunstane House, Midlothian (c.1672–5); Lethington House (now Lennoxlove House); Fast Lothian (1673–4 and 1676–7). Designed: Kinross House, Perth and Kinross (1686–93, for himself); Craigiehall House, West Lothian (c.1695–1708); and Hopetoun House, West Lothian (1699–1702 and 1706–10).

BURLINGTON, RICHARD BOYLE, (THIRD) EARL OF (1694–1753). Influential and very wealthy amateur architect of the (second) Palladian style. His only complete country house was Chiswick House, London (c.1725–9), but he added to and altered many others.

BURN, WILLIAM (1789–1870). Architect. Prolific Scottish Jacobethan architect who trained in Robert Smirke's office (1808–11) before returning to Edinburgh.

Harlaxton Manor, Lincs (completed following Salvin, from 1838); Falkland House, Fife (1839–44); Revesby Abbey, Lincs (1844); and Dartrey House, Co. Monaghan (1844–6, demolished in 1950 but Burn's stable block survives).

CAMPBELL, COLEN (1676–1729). Architect. Scottish lawyer and leader of the (second, post-Inigo Jones) Palladian movement. Published the first volume of *Vitruvius Britannicus* in 1715 (praising Palladio and Inigo Jones; second and third volumes 1717 and 1725) and the first book of Palladio's *Quattro Libri* in 1728. His first house was Wanstead House, Essex (1714–20, demolished 1824) which was the precedent for a century of Palladian and Neo-classical architecture.

Baldersby Park (originally Newby Park), N. Yorks (1720–8), Houghton Hall, Norfolk (begun 1722), Stourhead House, Wilts (1720–4), and Mereworth Castle, Kent (1722–5).

CARR, JOHN (1723–1807). Architect. Prolific Palladian, Neo-classical and occasionally Gothic architect practising mostly in Yorkshire and the North. Designed and added to public buildings, churches, innumerable bridges (he served as Bridgemaster for the North and West Ridings), town houses and country houses.

Harewood House, W. Yorks (1755–71); Tabley House, Ches (1760–7); Constable Burton Hall, N. Yorks (1762–8); stables at Castle Howard, N. Yorks (1774–82) and at Wentworth Woodhouse, W. Yorks (1766–89); and Middleton Lodge, N. Yorks (1777–80).

CARTER, THOMAS (?–1795). Sculptor. First employer of the sculptor Roubiliac. With his son, Thomas jnr., supplied many chimneypieces to Adam houses.

Croome Court, Worcs (1751–2); Shardeloes, Bucks (1758–66); Bowood House, Wilts (1762–76); Lansdowne House, London (1763–4, now the Lansdowne Club and much altered); and Syon House, London (1802–6).

CHAMBERS, SIR WILLIAM (1723–96). Neo-classical architect. Surveyor-General and Comptroller of the Works, 1769, Surveyor-General and Comptroller, 1782. Travelled in India and China (1740–9), studied in Italy (1750–5), and was thereafter advocate of all things Chinese (designed garden buildings at Kew, Surrey, and published *Designs of Chinese Buildings*, 1757) and Italian (*A Treatise on Civil Architecture*, 1759).

Duddingston House, Midlothian (1763–8) and Milton Abbey House, Dorset (1771–6). Also Somerset House, London (1776–96), and the theatre (1777–86) and chapel (1787–c.1800) at Trinity College, Dublin.

CHIPPENDALE, THOMAS (1718–79). Cabinet maker and designer. Worked as a journeyman cabinet maker in London before setting up his own business in the 1750s. This was continued by his son, also Thomas (1749–1822). In 1754 he became the first cabinet maker to publish his own designs as *The Gentleman and Cabinet Maker's*

Director, which was reprinted the same year and used by many other cabinet makers.

> Dumfries House, Ayrshire (1754–9); Blair Castle, Perth and Kinross (1758); Wilton House, Wilts (c.1759–73); Nostell Priory, W. Yorks (1766–85); Newby Hall, N. Yorks, (c.1772–76); Temple Newsam House, W. Yorks, (1774); Paxton House, Borders, (1774–91); Burton Constable Hall, E. Yorks (1768–79); and Petworth House, Sussex (1777–9).

CLARK, THOMAS (*fl.* 1742–82). Plasterer. Based at Westminster.

> Holkham Hall, Norfolk (1745–60, saloon, hall, various other rooms); and Ashburnham Place, Sussex (1760, now mostly demolished).

CLAYTON, THOMAS (*fl.* 1710–60) and his son, also Thomas (1743–93). Plasterers. Thomas Clayton senior was probably born in London, but he and his son worked entirely in Scotland.

> Hamilton Palace, Lanarkshire (c.1742–46, demolished 1921); Blair Castle, Perth and Kinross (1747–57); Glendoick, Perth and Kinross (c.1750, drawing room ceiling, staircase); Hopetoun House, West Lothian (c.1754, Yellow and Red drawing rooms); Dumfries House, Ayrshire (c.1756); and Yester House, East Lothian (c.1760, saloon).

CLEERE, WILLIAM (*fl.* 1668–90). Carver and joiner.

> Badminton House, Glos (1668), Hatley Park, Cambs (1683, wainscoting), and many London churches.

COADE, ELEANOR (1733–1821). Artificial stone maker. Daughter of George Coade and Eleanor Enchmarch, one of whom invented a stoneware body almost impervious to weathering and almost indistinguishable from limestone. She began manufacturing Coade Stone in Lambeth in 1769, producing architectural details (capitals, keystones), interior features (chimneypieces, tripods) and funerary monuments, and was soon used by every architect of note. Coade Stone went out of use c.1860.

COBB, JOHN (1710–78) and **VILE, WILLIAM** (c.1700–67). Cabinet makers. The partnership lasted from about 1751 to 1765. Appointed to royal service to George III and Queen Charlotte in 1751, and worked in that capacity until June 1763. Provided furniture of the highest quality to the royal palaces.

COLLINS, THOMAS (1735–1830). Plasterer. Londoner. Worked extensively for Sir William Chambers and became one of his executors and trustees.

Walcot Hall, Salop (1765); Milton Hall, Cambs (1771); Peper Harow House, Surrey (1777); and several London buildings, including Somerset House.

COLLINS, WILLIAM (1721–93). Plasterer and sculptor. Provided bas-reliefs, statues and many other features for Robert Adam.

Harewood House, W. Yorks (1760); Kedleston Hall, Derbys (1763); and Burton Constable Hall, E. Yorks (1769).

CORTESE, GIUSEPPE (*fl.* 1725–78). Stuccoist. From near Lugano. Settled in Yorkshire, working mostly for John Carr.

Newburgh Priory, N. Yorks (1739, 1743–5, 1764–7); Brandsby Hall, N. Yorks (1747–9); Gilling Castle, N. Yorks (c.1750); Elemore Hall, Durham (1752, 1757); Hardwick Hall, Durham (1757); Burton Constable, E. Yorks (1769); and Kilnwick House, E. Yorks (1772, mostly demolished 1951).

DANCE, GEORGE junior (1741–1825). Architect. Pioneer of Neo-classicism. Youngest son of a church architect, George Dance senior, who sent him to Italy for six years (1758–64) to study architecture. Extensive work in London (including Newgate Prison, 1770–80, demolished 1902).

Cranbury Park, Hants (c.1780, remodelled principal rooms); Camden Place, Kent (c.1788, 1807); Dorton House (formerly Wildernesse), Kent (c.1800, alterations); Mount Stewart, Co. Down (1804–5, west wing); Coleorton Hall, Leics (1804–8); and Kidbrooke Park, Sussex (1815, south front).

DAVIES, ROGER (*fl.* 1671–1709). Joiner. Nothing is known about him apart from his name.

Ragley Hall, Warwicks (c.1680); Burghley House, Lincs (1682–3); and Boughton House, Northants (1687–92). Also, Apothecaries' Hall, London (wainscoting and screen), Canterbury Cathedral (choir stalls), Chelsea Hospital, London and several city churches.

EDWARDS AND ROBERTS (Christian names and dates not known). Furniture manufacturers. A fashionable London firm founded in 1845. Made many high-quality pieces, both modern and reproductions. Based in Wardour and Oxford Streets, their work is often stamped on drawer edges with their name or bears their label. They ceased trading in 1899.

ELLIOTT, CHARLES (1752–1810). Cabinet maker. Supplied furniture to George III and Frederick, Duke of York. His furniture was elegantly made in satinwood in a late Neo-classical style. Much survives at Langleys, Essex (1721).

ENZER (or ENZIER), JOSEPH (*fl.* 1725–43). Plasterer. Said to have been Dutch. Worked for the Adam brothers at Arniston House, Midlothian (c.1730) and Yester House, East Lothian (1736–9; great staircase and dining room). Work in several other Adam houses is attributed to him.

FLITCROFT, HENRY (1697–1769). Carpenter, interior designer and a competent Palladian architect. Comptroller of the King's Works, Student of Inigo Jones and protégé of Lord Burlington.

Interiors of the hall, drawing room and dining rooms at Ditchley Park, Oxon (1724–5, 1736–40); interiors at St Giles House, Wimborne St Giles, Dorset (1740–4); interiors and south front of Milton Hall, Cambs (1750–1); east front and wings of Wentworth Woodhouse, S. Yorks (c.1735–c.1770), reckoned to be the longest Palladian frontage in England; and Woburn Abbey, Beds (1747–61).

FRANCHINI (or FRANCINI), PAUL and PHILIP (*fl.* 1730–60). Stuccoists. Italian. There may have been three of them working in England and Ireland.

Wallington Hall, Northumb (1740–1, dining room and saloon) and several houses in Ireland such as Castletown House, Co. Kildare (1722–9).

FUHRLOHG, CHRISTOPHER (c.1737–85). Cabinet maker and marquetry maker. Swedish. Came to London, via Amsterdam and Paris, before 1767, and later described himself on his trade cards as 'Ebéniste to his Royal Highness the Prince of Wales'. Supplied marquetry panels to other cabinet makers.

GIBBONS, GRINLING (1648–1721). Woodcarver and sculptor. Master Carver in Wood to the Crown. Born in Rotterdam of English parents, came to England in about 1667 and was introduced to Charles II. Worked with Sir Christopher Wren at St Paul's Cathedral and at several city churches. His work, in both wood and stone, is in many country houses.

Sudbury Hall, Derbys (1660s); Belton House, Lincs (1685–8); Dunham Massey Hall, Ches (1732–40); and Petworth House, Sussex (1688).

GIBBS, JAMES (1682–1754). Architect. Sent to train for the priesthood in Rome in 1703, he determined to become an architect. Returned to England in 1709 with a thorough knowledge of Italian Baroque and a deep admiration for Sir Christopher Wren. Published *A Book of*

Architecture (1728), possibly the most widely read book on the subject in the eighteenth century.

Sudbrooke House, Surrey (c.1717–20); Patshull Hall, Staffs (c.1730); Ditchley Park, Oxon (c.1722); alterations to Wimpole Hall, Cambs (1719–21), Fairlawne, Kent (c.1722), and others. Also designed St Mary-le-Strand (1714–24), St Martin-in-the-Fields (1722–6), the Senate House (1722–30) and the Fellows' Building, King's College, (1724–49) Cambridge, and the Radcliffe Camera (1737–8), Oxford.

GILBERT, JOHN (*fl.* mid-eighteenth century). Carver. Londoner. Worked frequently for Robert Adam.

Croome Court, Worcs (1767), Mersham-le-Hatch, Kent (1768, door cases, overmantels), and Shardeloes, Bucks (1758–66).

GILPIN, WILLIAM SAWREY (1762–1843). Watercolour artist (first President, Society of Painters in Water Colours, 1804), teacher (Royal Military College, Sandhurst, 1806–20) and landscape gardener (c.1820–43). He continued the Picturesque movement.

Scotney Castle, Kent (1837); Hawarden Castle, Flints (1752); and Nuneham Park, Oxon (1756), where he laid out the Pinetum, which formed the core of the Harcourt Arboretum.

GIMSON, ERNEST WILLIAM (1864–1919). Furniture maker. Joined the Arts and Crafts movement after meeting the Barnsley brothers, with whom he formed the firm of Kenton and Co. (Gimson, Sidney Barnsley, W. R. Lethaby). Gimson and the Barnsleys moved to the Cotswolds in 1893, and by 1903 all three had settled at Sapperton. Gimson produced furniture of fine proportions and excellent construction. He employed professional cabinet makers, unlike his friend Sidney Barnsley, who executed his own designs.

His work may be seen at Rodmarton Manor, Glos (1909–29), Owlpen Manor, Glos (1616), and in museums at Leicester, Cheltenham and Bath (Holburne Museum).

GOODISON, BENJAMIN (c.1700–67). Royal cabinet maker to George II (1727 onwards).

St James's Palace and Hampton Court Palace, both London; Blenheim Palace, Oxon (1740 onwards, for the Duchess of Marlborough); Longford Castle, Wilts (1737 onwards, for Viscount Folkestone); Holkham Hall, Norfolk (for the Earl of Leicester); and Deene Park, Northants (for the Earl of Cardigan).

GOUDGE (GOUGE), EDWARD (late seventeenth–early eighteenth centuries). Plasterer. Worked for Nicholas Hawksmoor and William Winde.

Coombe Abbey, Warwicks (1682–3); Thoresby Hall, Notts (1686); Belton House, Lincs (1688); Castle Bromwich Hall, W. Mid (1688–90); Swallowfield Park, Berks (1690–1); Petworth House, Sussex (1691–2); and Chatsworth House, Derbys (1696–7).

GRAHAM, GEORGE (1673–1751). Clockmaker. Pupil and partner of Thomas Tompion. Master of the Clockmakers' Company from 1722. Invented the mercury pendulum for more accurate timekeeping.

GRENDEY, GILES (1693–1780). Cabinet maker. Born in Gloucestershire and came to London in 1719. Had extensive workshops in Clerkenwell and a large export business in Chinese style and scarlet-japanned furniture. Master of the Joiners' Company from 1766.

GROVE, JOHN (?–1676) and **JOHN II** (?–1708). Plasterers. Father and son.

Queen's House, London (1661, ceiling, east bridge room); Badminton House, Glos (1682); Cornbury Park, Oxon (1664, attributed); and Easton Neston, Northants (c.1690, attributed).

HAWKSMOOR, NICHOLAS (1661–1736). Baroque architect, mainly of churches and public buildings. Worked with Wren c.1684–1700 on St Paul's Cathedral and other projects.

Blenheim Palace, Oxon (Vanbrugh's assistant, 1705–16; in sole charge, 1722–5; Triumphal Gateway, 1722–3); Castle Howard, N. Yorks (the Pyramid, 1728; the Mausoleum, 1729–36); and Easton Neston, Northants (c.1695–1702).

HENDERSON, JAMES (*fl.* 1755–87). Plasterer from York. Associated with John Carr.

Harewood House, W. Yorks (1765); Swinton Park, N. Yorks (1766); Cannon Hall, S. Yorks (1766–7); Kirkleatham Hall, N. Yorks (1767, demolished 1954); Temple Newsam House, W. Yorks (1771); Gilling Castle, N. Yorks (1771); and Thirsk Hall, N. Yorks (1773).

HEAL, SIR AMBROSE (1872–1959). Furniture manufacturer. Showed that well-designed furniture could be made available at a reasonable price. Entered the family firm of Heal & Son in 1893, and issued his first catalogue of oak bedroom furniture in 1898. He designed hand- and machine-made furniture.

HEPPLEWHITE, GEORGE (c.1727–86). Furniture designer. Very few biographical facts are known. Apparently apprenticed to Gillows in Lancaster and later moved to London and opened a cabinet maker's shop. No furniture made by him or his firm is known to exist and his reputation is based on designs in *The Cabinet-Maker and Upholsterer's Guide*, published posthumously in 1788 by his wife Alice. The Hepplewhite 'style' (popular from about 1775–1800) was slender, light and elegant, and his chairs were characteristic for their shield backs.

HOBCROFT (or **HOBCRAFT**), **JOHN** (*fl.* 1730–79). Joiner, builder and occasionally architect.

> Stowe House, Bucks (1755), Croome Court, Worcs (1758–64), and Corsham Court, Wilts (1766). Designed the chapel at Audley End, Cambs (1768); Padworth House, Berks (1769); and Wasing House, Berks (1772, destroyed by fire 1945).

HOLLAND, HENRY (1745–1806). Architect and urban planner. Partner and son-in-law of 'Capability' Brown, with whom he built Claremont House, Surrey (1771–4). Made his name with Brooks's, St James's Street, London (1776–8). The Prince Regent's initial architect (later replaced by John Nash) for the Royal Pavilion, Brighton, Sussex (1786–7). His urban planning projects included parts of Knightsbridge and Chelsea (the Hans Town project, from 1777) and the Albany (from 1802) where he converted and extended Melbourne House into sixty-nine apartments.

> Designed Berrington Hall, Herefs (1778–81). Major alterations to Broadlands, Hants (1788–92), Woburn Abbey, Beds (1787–1802), Althorp, Northants (1787–9), and Southill Park, Beds (1796–1800). Major remodelling of Carlton House, Pall Mall, London (1783–96, demolished 1825). {Trentham Park see Brown P.13}

HOLLAND AND SONS. Cabinet makers and upholsterers. Founded in 1803 by William Holland (*fl.* 1803–43) in partnership with Stephen Taprell, becoming Holland and Sons in 1843. They employed 350 men by 1851 and had a fashionable clientele, working for Queen Victoria at Buckingham Palace, Balmoral and Osborne House and furnishing the Athenaeum Club in Pall Mall.

HOPPER, THOMAS (1776–1856). Architect. Fashionable and supremely eclectic designer: 'to understand all styles and to be prejudiced in favour of none.' Many of his houses have been altered or destroyed.

> Leigh Court, Som (1814, Palladian), Gosford Castle, Co. Armagh (1819–21, pseudo-Norman), Penrhyn Castle, Gwynedd (1822–37, also pseudo-

Norman), Danbury Place, Essex (1832, Tudorbethan), and Wivenhoe Park, Essex (1846–9, Jacobethan).

INCE AND MAYHEW. Furniture makers. William Ince (1738–1804) and John Mayhew (1736–1811) entered into partnership in 1759 and produced fine Neo-classical furniture. They issued their folio design book *The Universal System of Household Furniture* (modelled on Chippendale's *The Gentleman and Cabinet-Maker's Director*) in 1759–62, with a dedication to one of their principal patrons, the Duke of Marlborough.

Croome Court, Worcs; Audley End, Essex; Crichel House, Dorset; Daylesford House, Glos; and Chatsworth House, Derbys.

JEKYLL, GERTRUDE (1843–1932). Garden designer and writer. She was a pioneer of horticulture (much influenced by William Robinson) and of the informal, cottage-garden style. Designed some 300 gardens, a third of which were designed for Lutyens.

Munstead Wood, Surrey (1896–9, for a time her home); The Deanery, Berks (1899–1901); Orchards, Munstead, Surrey (1897–9); and Barrington Court, Som (1920s).

JENSEN, GERRIT or **GERREIT** (*fl.* 1680–d.1715). Cabinet maker. Craftsman of Dutch or Flemish extraction working in England. His furniture echoes the French style. He provided marquetry furniture for William and Mary (Windsor Castle, Berks). From 1689 he was principal supplier to the Royal Wardrobe 'of writing-desks, pier-glasses, stands and card-tables'.

Kensington Palace and Hampton Court Palace, both in London; Boughton House and Deene Park, both in Northants; Chatsworth House, Derbys; Knole Park, Kent; Burghley House, Lincs; Petworth House, Sussex; and Clandon Park, Surrey.

JONES, INIGO (1573–1652). Surveyor of the King's Works, 1613. Introduced the Palladian style to England. His work as a country house architect is now mostly suspect.

Queen's House (1616–35); Banqueting House, Whitehall (1619–22); Queen's Chapel, St James's (1623–5); remodelling of St Paul's Cathedral (1625–40); and St Paul's Church, Covent Garden (1631–3). All in London.

KAUFFMANN, ANGELICA (1741–1807). Historical and portrait painter. Swiss. Introduced in London in 1766 and stayed until 1781, when she left for Rome. Her name is erroneously attached to many ceiling paintings and much painted furniture. She was employed by Robert Adam, along with her second husband, Antonio Zucchi, and provided coloured engravings to Matthew Boulton for his 'Mechanical Paintings' process. Many of these survive on commodes, chair backs, etc.

KENT, WILLIAM (c.1685–1748). Architect (after 1730), landscape architect, painter, and interior and furniture designer. Protégé of Lord Burlington. As a landscape architect, he was a pioneer of the Picturesque. Designed furniture for several of his houses, such as Rousham House, Oxon, and for other buildings, such as Hampton Court Palace, London.

> Burlington House, Chiswick House, and Kensington Palace (all London, painted ceilings); Claremont House, Surrey (gardens 1715–27); Holkham Hall, Norfolk (1734–65), a purely Palladian country house; Rousham House, Oxon (gardens 1740s); Stowe House, Bucks (gardens 1740s); and fabriques at Stowe House, Bucks (c.1730–5); built the Treasury Building (1733–7) and the Horse Guards Building (1748–59), both in London.

KNIBB, JOSEPH (1640–1711). Clockmaker. The most famous of an eminent clockmaking family, which included his father Samuel (to whom he was apprenticed), his younger brother John, and his cousin Peter. Clockmaker to Charles I and James II. Worked first at Oxford (1662–70), where he probably built the first working anchor escapement clock, and then in London. Three fine clocks by him are at Lyme Park, Ches and one at Trerice, Cornwall.

LAGUERRE, LOUIS (1663–1721). Decorative painter. French, godson of Louis XIV. Came to England about 1684.

> Chatsworth House, Derbys (1689–94, chapel, hall, music room, state bedroom); Sudbury Hall, Derbys (c.1692); Burghley House, Lincs (1698, ballroom walls); Hampton Court Palace, London (c.1699); Wollaton Hall, Notts (c.1699, great hall, staircase); Ampthill Park House, Beds (before 1706); Petersham House, Surrey (c.1710); Cannons, London (before 1715, staircase ceiling, burnt 1747); Petworth House, Surrey (after 1714, staircase); and Blenheim Palace, Oxon (c.1720, saloon).

LANGLOIS, PIERRE (*fl.* 1738–c.1770). Cabinet maker. French. Settled in Tottenham Court Road, London, in the 1750s. The earliest dated reference to his work in England is 1759. He became famous for commodes and writing-tables, supplying them to the royal family, the Dukes of Bedford and Northumberland and the Earl of Coventry.

He was noted for the care with which he treated even the interiors of his pieces.

LEONI, GIACOMO (c.1686–1746). Architect. Came to England (from Venice? via Dusseldorf) about 1713 and published first English edition of Palladio's *Quattro Libri*, creating an instant revival of interest in Palladianism.

Clandon Park, Surrey (c.1730-3); Alkrington Hall, Lancs (1735-6); and major alterations to Lyme Park, Ches (c.1725-35).

LIMINGE (LYMINGE, LEMYINGE), ROBERT (d. 1628). Architect and builder. He was a carpenter by trade and little is known of him.

Hatfield House, Herts (1607-12, gardens by John Tradescant the elder) and Blickling Hall, Norfolk (1616-17). Both houses are in the Jacobean style.

LINNELL, WILLIAM (c.1702–63) and **JOHN** (1729–96). Cabinet makers, father and son. They had a successful business, firstly in the Rococo style, including a commission from the fourth Duke of Beaufort at Badminton House (the Badminton bed), and then in the Neo-classical style under John's supervision (e.g. furniture at Dyrham Park, Glos and Crichel House, Dorset).

LONDON, GEORGE (c.1640–1714). Master Gardener and Deputy Superintendent of the Royal Gardens.

Melbourne Hall, Derbys (partly survives); Blenheim Palace (the east parterre, recreated); Hampton Court Palace (the Privy garden, recreated); Chatsworth House, Derbys, Longleat House, Wilts, and Wimpole Hall, Cambs, all in partnership with Henry Wise.

LUTYENS, SIR EDWIN LANDSEER (1869–1944). Architect. Set up his own practice in 1888. His first commission was Crooksbury, Surrey (1889) where he met Gertrude Jekyll, a lifelong colleague who designed about one hundred gardens for his country houses. Followed the Arts and Crafts style until about 1990 and then adopted many traditional styles.

Crooksbury, Surrey (1889), Fulbrook House, Surrey (1897-9), Orchards, Surrey (1897-9), and The Pleasaunce, Norfolk (1880s), all Arts and Crafts; Heathcote, W. Yorks (1906-8), a mixture of Art and Crafts and Neo-classical; Tigbourne Court, Surrey (1899-1901) and Homewood, Herts (1901), Neo-classical; Little Thakeham, Sussex (1902), and Overstrand Hall, Norfolk (1901), Tudor; Folly Farm, Berks (1906) and The Salutation, Kent (1911),

William and Mary; Nashdom, Bucks (1905–8), Georgian; and Castle Drogo, Devon (1910–32, probably the last castle to be built in the UK), pseudo-Mediaeval. Architect of the Cenotaph, London (1920), of New Delhi (from 1912) and the Imperial War Graves Commission (from 1917). Mainly public buildings from c.1920.

MACKINTOSH, CHARLES RENNIE (1868–1928). Watercolourist, interior and furniture designer, and Art Nouveau architect. His architectural career lasted only ten years (1896–1906). Worked mostly on public buildings and seems to have designed only two country houses: Windy Hill, Renfrewshire (1899–1902) and The Hill House, Argyll and Bute (1903), for which he also designed the furniture. Other examples of his furniture and interior design are housed in the Hunterian Art Gallery, University of Glasgow.

MAINE (MAYNE), JONATHAN (*fl.* 1680–1709). Carver.

Burghley House, Lincs (1682–5); Kiveton Hall, W. Yorks (1703–4, demolished 1812); St Paul's Cathedral (1696–1709); Trinity College Chapel, Oxford (1695); and several London churches.

MANSFIELD, ISAAC (*fl.* 1697–1739). Plasterer. Worked for several eminent architects, including Vanbrugh, Hawksmoor, Burlington and Kent.

Castle Howard, N. Yorks (1710); Chicheley Hall, Bucks (1721, hall and staircase); Langleys, Essex (1721, hall); Houghton Hall, Norfolk (1725–9); Goodwood House, Sussex (1725); Blenheim Palace, Oxon (1725, long library, chapel); Claremont House, Surrey (1730, drawing room); Kew Palace, Surrey (1730); and Raynham Hall, Norfolk (c.1730, attributed).

MAROT, DANIEL (1661–1752). Baroque architect, decorator and furniture designer. French Huguenot who left France for Holland where he entered the service of the future William III. Marot followed William III to England in 1688 and made at least three visits to England in the next ten years. Worked extensively at Hampton Court Palace. His engraved designs (published 1712) had an important influence, especially on the work of cabinet makers. He also designed clocks and gilded leatherwork. He left England for Holland around 1698.

MARTIN (MARTYN), EDWARD (*fl.* 1648–99). Plasterer.

Arbury Hall, Warwicks (1678, chapel ceiling) and Burghley House, Lincs (1682).

MAYHEW, JOHN, see INCE, William.

MILLER, SANDERSON (1716–80). Gentleman architect and leader of the Gothic Revival. Added Gothic features to his own house, Radway Grange, Warwicks (1744–6), and was consulted about many more.

'Ruined' castles at Hagley Hall, Worcs (1747–8) and at Wimpole Hall, Cambs (1749–51); the great hall and Gothic gateway at Lacock Abbey, Wilts (1754–5); and windows at Arbury Hall, Warwicks (c.1750–2).

MOORE (MOOR), ROBERT (*fl.* 1745–74). Plasterer. Lived at Warwick.

Radway Grange, (c.1745); Alscot Park, (1750–2, staircase, great hall ceiling); Arbury Hall, (1755, library); and Stoneleigh Abbey, (c.1760). All in Warwicks.

MORRIS, ROGER (1695–1749). Palladian and Gothic Revival architect. His most important houses are listed below but he added to and altered many more.

Clearwell Castle, Glos (1728, Gothic) and Inveraray Castle, Argyll and Bute (1745–60, Gothic)

MORRIS, WILLIAM (1834–96). Poet, translator, painter, designer and manufacturer. The main inspiration of the Arts and Crafts Movement. Helped to found Morris, Marshall Faulkner & Co. in 1861 making stained glass, textiles, wallpapers, furniture, tapestries and carpets. The original firm was dissolved in 1874, but continued under several names, including Morris and Co.

His works may be seen at: Wightwick Manor, W. Mid (first phase completed 1887, great parlour wing in 1893); Standen, Sussex (1892–4); and Kelmscott Manor, Oxon (about 1570, Morris's home 1871–96).

MORRISON, SIR RICHARD (1767–1849). Irish Neo-classical and Gothic Revival architect.

Bearforest, Co. Cork (1807–8) and Castlegar, Co. Galway (from 1801). Collaborated with his son, W. V. Morrison, on Ballyfin, Co. Leix (1822), Baronscourt, Co. Tyrone (1835), Borris House, Co. Carlow (c.1813), Fota Island, Co. Cork (c.1825), and Shelton Abbey, Co. Wicklow (1819).

MORRISON, WILLIAM VITRUVIUS (1794–1838). Irish Neo-classical and Tudorbethan architect, son of Sir Richard Morrison, with whom he collaborated.

Clontarf Castle, Co. Dublin (1836–7), Glenarm Castle, Co. Antrim (1823–4), and Hollybrook House, Co. Wicklow (1835), all Tudorbethan; Mount Stewart, Co. Down (1825–8, Neo-classical).

MUDGE, THOMAS (1715–94). Clockmaker. Apprentice of George Graham. Set up his own business in 1748. Around 1755 he invented the detached lever escapement, which continues to be a component of watches today. In 1771, due to ill-health, he moved to Plymouth and from this date worked on the development of a marine chronometer. In 1776 he was appointed watchmaker to King George III.

NASH, JOHN (1752–1835). Picturesque architect and city planner. Trained in the office of Sir Robert Taylor. Set up on his own (1775) but on inheriting a fortune gave up architecture. Bankrupted in 1783 through bad investments and retired to Wales. Took up architecture again. His country houses are largely, although by no means solely, in and around Wales and, although it is not known when, if ever, he visited the country, in Ireland. Returned to London 1796, formed partnership with Humphrey Repton (dissolved 1802). The Prince Regent's favourite architect. In London his work was extensive. He designed Regent's Park and the buildings around it including Regent Street, All Souls, Langham Place, Buckingham Palace, Carlton House Terrace and Marble Arch.

> Killymoon Castle, Co. Tyrone (c.1801–3); Ffynone, Pembs (1792–6); Cronkhill, Salop (c.1802); Longner Hall, Salop (c.1805); alterations to Attingham Park, Salop (1807–10); Caerhays Castle, Cornwall (1808); Lough Cutra Castle, Co. Galway (1811); Gracefield Lodge, Co. Kildare (1817); and the Royal Pavilion, Sussex (1815–22).

NEEDHAM, JOSHUA (*fl.* 1721–25). Plasterer.

> Chicheley Hall, Bucks (1721); Sutton Scarsdale Hall, Derbys (1724, ruined 1919–20); and Ditchley Park, Oxon (1724).

NELSON, SAFFRON or **SEFFERIN** (*fl.* 1775–89). Carver/gilder. Worked on many Robert Adam commissions.

> Croome Court, Worcs (1781); Chatsworth House, Derbys (1782); and Carlton House, London (1789, demolished 1825).

NESFIELD, WILLIAM ANDREWS. (1793–1881). Soldier and landscape architect. Father of W. E. Nesfield and brother-in-law of Anthony Salvin. Fought in the Peninsular War and at Waterloo. Retired in 1816 and began to work as a landscape architect.

> Witley Court, Worcs (fountains and south parterre), Castle Howard, N. Yorks (south lake, Prince of Wales fountain, cascade, and waterfall); Oxon

Hoath, Kent (formal gardens); Treberfydd, Powys (long walk); and Kinmel Hall, Den (walled gardens), Trentham Park (vast parterre connecting house & lake)

NESFIELD, WILIAM EDEN (1835–88). Architect. Son of W. A Nesfield. Partner (1862–76) of Norman Shaw. Designed in the Gothic Revival tradition and later on instigated the Queen Anne Style.

Cloverley Hall, Salop (1864–70, largely rebuilt 1926); Kinmel Hall, Den (1866–74); additions to Bodrhyddan Hall, Flints (1872–4), and Loughton Hall, Essex (1878).

PAINE, JAMES (1717–89). Palladian architect and member of the Burlington circle. Designed and altered many country houses.

Kedleston Hall, Derbys (1759–60), where he was superseded by Robert Adam; the stables at Chatsworth House, Derbys (c.1760); the Temple of Diana and the 'Roman Bridge', Weston Park, Staffs (1765–70); New Wardour Castle, Wilts (1770–6); Sandbeck Park, S. Yorks (1763–8); and Thorndon Hall, Essex (1764–70).

PAXTON, SIR JOSEPH (1803–65). Gardener and self-taught architect. Head gardener at Chatsworth House, Derbys, 1826–56, where he improved the gardens and designed conservatories. Made his reputation with the 'Great Stove' conservatory at Chatsworth (1836–40, destroyed 1920). Created the village of Edensor, near Chatsworth (1838–48).

Mentmore Towers, Bucks (1854); Battlesden House, Beds (1864); and the Crystal Palace (1850–1, originally in Hyde Park, later relocated to Sydenham). Public parks included Prince's Park, Liverpool (1842), Birkenhead Park (1847), Baxter Park, Dundee (1863), Kelvingrove Park, Glasgow (1856), and People's Park, Halifax (1856–7).

PEARCE, SIR EDWARD LOVETT (c.1699–1733). Architect. A brief career which earned him the title of the father of Palladianism in Ireland. Went to Italy, 1722–4. Surveyor General of Ireland, 1731–33.

Castletown House, Co. Kildare (c.1726–7, following Galilei); Bellamont House, Co. Cavan (c.1729); south elevation of Drumcondra House, Co. Dublin (1727); Cashel Palace, Co. Tipperary (c.1727–32); and Parliament House, Dublin (from 1729, completed by Arthur Dobbs). May have worked on Castle Howard with his father's cousin, Sir John Vanbrugh.

PEARCE, WILLIAM (*fl.* 1762–72). Plasterer.

Bowood House, Wilts (1762–76); Claremont House, Surrey (1772); and Berrington Hall, Herefs (1772, attributed).

PERRITT, THOMAS (1710–59). Plasterer. Yorkshireman working mainly in the north of England.

Raby Castle, Durham (1738–53); Temple Newsam House, W. Yorks (1741–7, long gallery, library); Kilnwick House, E. Yorks (1749); and Nostell Priory, W. Yorks (c.1740, dining room, music room, north and south staircases).

PERRITT, WILLIAM (*fl.* 1724–70). Plasterer, probably brother of Thomas.

Newby Hall, N. Yorks (1724–8); Studley Royal House, N. Yorks (1728, destroyed by fire 1946); Farnborough Hall, Warwicks (1750); and Blair Castle, Perth and Kinross (1755).

PRATT, SIR ROGER (1620–85). Architect. Pioneer of Neo-classicism in England. He designed only five houses.

Coleshill, Berks (c.1650–62, demolished 1952); Kingston Lacy, Dorset (1663–5, altered by Barry 1835–9); Horseheath, Cambs (1663–5, demolished 1792); Ryston Hall, Norfolk, his own home (1669–72, altered by Soane 1786–8); and Clarendon House, Picadilly, London (1664–7, demolished 1683).

PRESCOTT, RICHARD (?–1747). Carver. From Liverpool.

Croxteth Hall, Lancs (1702, wainscoting) and Woolton Hall, Lancs (c.1709, wainscoting).

PUGIN, AUGUSTUS WELBY NORTHMORE (1812–52). Architect and central figure of the Gothic Revival. Mostly churches and public buildings.

Alton Towers (from 1837, partly ruinous) and Alton Castle (1840–52), both in Staffs; Scarisbrick Hall, Lancs (1836–47); Bilton Grange, Warwicks (1841); and Wilburton Manor House, Cambs (1848).

REPTON, HUMPHRY (1752–1818). Picturesque landscape architect. He created 'red books' for prospective clients in which 'before' and 'after' views were illustrated.

Burley-on-the-Hill House, Rut (1795), Corsham Court, Wilts (1796–1800), Attingham Park, Salop (1798), Luscombe Castle, Devon (1799) and Ashridge House, Herts (1814), all in partnership with John Nash. May have helped his son John with the design of Sheringham Hall, Norfolk (1812–19).

RICHARDS, JAMES (*fl.* 1718–59). Master carpenter and carver. Succeeded (1721) Grinling Gibbons as Master Sculptor and Carver in Wood at the Office of Works. Worked on many projects in London.

Chicheley Hall, Bucks (1722, garden front rooms); Goodwood House, Sussex (c.1725); Compton Place, Sussex (1728–31, staircase doors); and Houghton Hall, Norfolk (c.1729).

ROBERTS, THOMAS (1711–71). Plasterer. From Oxford. Worked extensively at university and college buildings in the city.

Ditchley Park, Oxon (1749, 1760); Hartwell House, Bucks (1764); Rousham House, Oxon (1764, great parlour); Pusey House, Berks (c.1748); The Menagerie, Northants (c.1749); Honington Hall, Warwicks (c.1753–8); and Nuthall Temple, Notts (1769).

ROBINSON, WILLIAM (1838–1935). Horticulturalist, landscape gardener and writer. Visited France, Italy and the USA. Wrote *Alpine flowers for English gardens* and *The Wild Garden* (both 1870), which helped to popularise hardy plants in natural settings. Founded *The Garden* (1871) and *Gardening Illustrated* (1879), both very successful magazines. Published *The English Flower Garden* in 1883. Created his model garden at Gravetye Manor, Sussex (1598). A great friend of, and influence on, Gertrude Jekyll.

ROSE, JOSEPH (c.1723–80). Plasterer. Apprenticed to Thomas Perritt and later worked with his brother Jonathan and nephews Joseph and Jonathan. Together they formed the firm of Joseph Rose & Co. which secured most of the important commissions of this era.

Wentworth Woodhouse, S. Yorks (1751–63, great hall, dining room, drawing room, writing room etc); Felbrigg Hall, Norfolk (c.1752); Ormesby Hall, N. Yorks (1755); and Nostell Priory, W. Yorks (c.1740, north and south staircase, dining room, music room).

ROSE, JOSEPH (1745–99). Plasterer. Son of Joseph's brother Jonathan.

Shardeloes, Bucks (1761–3); Croome Court, Worcs (1762); Chatsworth House, Derbys (c.1763); Audley End, Cambs (1763–5, and at intervals until 1786); Mersham-le-Hatch, Kent (1766, great drawing room and great dining room ceilings); Claydon House, Bucks (1767–8, staircase, ceilings); Ampthill Park House, Beds (1769, drawing room ceiling); Newby Hall, N. Yorks (1771, dining room, hall ceiling); and Kedleston Hall, Derbys (?1775, music room, drawing room, library, dining room, saloon, hall, portico). The firm also carried out substantial commissions in London.

RUSSELL, SIR GORDON (1892–1980). Furniture designer and artist-craftsman. He worked in the Cotswold School traditions of Gimson and the Barnsley brothers. Set up a firm in Broadway, Worcs (1923), which made some of the best hand- and machine-made modern furniture, eventually employing over 200 workmen. Turned to industrial methods, including the design of radio cabinets for mass production. In the Second World War became design chairman of the Utility Design programme (1943–7). Later played a major part in the Festival of Britain (1952) and was director of the Design Council (1947–59).

SALVIN, ANTHONY (1799–1881). Revivalist architect. He added to and altered many country houses, castles, cathedrals and churches.

Mamhead Park, Devon (1826–38, in the Tudor style); Harlaxton Manor, Lincs (1831–8, Jacobethan); Scotney Castle, Kent (1835, Jacobethan); Peckforton Castle, Ches (1844–50, a recreation of a thirteenth century castle); and Thoresby Hall, Notts (1864–75, Jacobethan).

SEDDON, GEORGE (1727–1801). Cabinet maker and furniture seller. Master of the Joiners' Company from 1795. He set up in London sometime before 1750 and established London's first furniture showroom, with workshops attached. He employed over 400 craftsmen (most of them specialists) and apprentices, and also relied on the 'slop trade' (cheap home-workers). His sons George and Thomas entered into partnership in 1785 and 1788 respectively, and in 1793 his son-in-law, Thomas Shackleton, joined them. The firm was wound up in 1868.

SHAW, (RICHARD) NORMAN (1831–1912). Architect in a variety of revivalist styles: Gothic, Jacobethan, Queen Anne (with W. E. Nesfield), and vernacular. Joined Salvin's office (1856) and then Street's (1858). In 1863 set up a partnership with W. E. Nesfield. .

Glen Andred, Sussex (1866–8); Leys Wood, Sussex (1868–9, mostly destroyed); Cragside, Northumb (1870–84); Preen Manor, Salop (1870–1, mostly destroyed); Bourton Manor, Salop (1874); Adcote, Salop (1876–81); Bryanston House, Dorset (1889–94); and Chesters House, Northumb (1890s).

SHERATON, THOMAS (1751–1806). Furniture designer. Born in Stockton-on-Tees, trained as a journeyman cabinet maker and moved to London in 1790 as a consultant and teacher. In 1791 he published *The Cabinet-Maker and Upholsterer's Drawing Book* (four volumes, 1791–4) which was immediately influential. He followed this with *The Cabinet Dictionary* (1803) and *Cabinet-Maker, Upholsterer and General Artist's Encyclopaedia* (1805). He returned to Stockton around 1802 and was ordained as a Baptist minister. No piece definitely made by Sheraton—if he made any—has survived, and, like Hepplewhite, his reputation is based on his designs.

SIMPSON, ARTHUR WILLIAM (1857–1922). Carver and furniture maker. An Arts and Crafts furniture maker who settled in Kendal. He worked on his own account and with many architects, making a wide range of domestic and ecclesiastical furniture.

SMIRKE, SIR ROBERT (1780–1867). Neo-classical and occasionally Gothic Revival architect. Official architect to the Office of Works (with John Nash and Sir John Soane), 1813.

> Lowther Castle, Cumb (1806–14, interior gutted in 1940s and 1957); Wilton Castle, N. Yorks (c.1810); Eastnor Castle, Herefs (1812–20); and Normanby Hall, Lincs (1825–30) — all Gothic Revival. Mostly public buildings in London: British Museum (1823–31); Canada House (1824–7, previously the Royal College of Physicians building); and Oxford and Cambridge Club (1837).

SMITH, FRANCIS (1672–1738) and **WILLIAM** (1661–1724). Builders and architects. Sons of Francis Smith, bricklayer, of Tettenhall, Staffs. Francis was trained as a mason and William as a bricklayer; Francis moved to Warwick and William stayed at his father's house. Jointly and separately they designed or built many churches, including St Mary's Warwick. Their many country houses are run-of-the-mill Queen Anne style, but the brothers were renowned for their good craftsmanship and honesty. Many have been demolished or greatly altered.

> Umberslade Hall, Warwicks (1693–1700); Stanford Hall, Leics (1697–1700); Cottesbrooke Hall, Northants (1703–13); Heythrop Park, Oxon (c.1705–8, designed by Thomas Archer); Chettle House, Dorset (c.1715–20, also designed by Thomas Archer); Chicheley Hall, Bucks (1719–20); Ditchley Park, Oxon (1720–42, designed by James Gibbs); Davenport House, Salop (c.1726); and Kinlet Hall, Salop (1727–9).

SMYTHSON, ROBERT (c.1535–1614). Stonemason and 'Surveyor' (architect).

> Longleat House, Wilts (1568–75, stonemason); Wollaton Hall, Notts (1580–88); Hardwick Hall, Derbys (1590–7); Doddington Hall, Lincs (c.1595); and Burton Agnes Hall, E. Yorks (1601–10).

SMYTHSON, JOHN (c.1570–1634). Stonemason. Son of Robert, with whom he initially worked.

> Bolsover Castle, Derbys (c.1612–34); Welbeck Abbey, Notts (1622–3); and perhaps Slingsby Castle, N. Yorks (c.1630, left unfinished c.1645).

SOANE, SIR JOHN (1753–1837). Neo-classical architect. Trained under Dance the Younger and Henry Holland. Travelled in Italy. Made his name with his Bank of England.

> Letton Hall, Norfolk (1783–9); Chillington Hall, Staffs (1785, following Francis Smith); Moggerhanger House, Beds (1790–3); Wimpole Hall, Cambs (1790s, after James Gibbs and Henry Flitcroft); Tyringham Hall, Bucks (1792); Pitzhanger Manor, Ealing, London (1800–4, his own house; at that time Ealing was in the country); Aynhoe Park, Oxon (1800–5); Pell Wall Hall, Salop (1822–8, gutted 1986); and Wotton House, Bucks (1820s).

STANLEY, CHARLES (1703–61). Plasterer. Born in Copenhagen of English parents, resident in England from 1727 until 1746 when he returned to Denmark.

> Langley Hall, Norfolk (c.1740, saloon); Okeover Hall, Staffs (c.1745); Compton Place, Sussex (1728–9, attributed); and Kirtlington Park, Oxon (c.1745).

STEUART, GEORGE (c.1730–1806). Neo-classical architect. A Gaelic-speaking Highlander, many of whose works are in Shropshire.

> Attingham Park, Salop (1783–5, with gardens by Humphrey Repton, later altered internally by John Nash); the Ionic Temple at Millichope Park, Salop (1770); Baronscourt, Co. Tyrone (1779–82, remodelled by Soane and Morrison); and Castle Mona, Douglas, Isle of Man (1801–6). Also St Chad's, Shrewsbury, Salop (1790–2) and All Saints, Wellington, Salop (1787–9).

STUART, JAMES 'ATHENIAN' (1713–88). Architect. A central figure in the Greek Revival. Visited Italy (1742, 1748) and Greece (1751–5). Published with Nicholas Revett *The Antiquities of Athens, Measured and Delineated* (1762, second volume 1789), which was at once recognized as authoritative. Designed little due to idleness.

Garden buildings at Hagley Hall, Worcs (1758) and Shugborough Hall, Staffs (1760s), reputed to be the first houses in eighteenth century Europe to have Greek orders; and the Tower of the Winds, Mount Stewart, Co. Down (1782–3).

SWAN, ABRAHAM (*fl.* 1733–59). Carpenter, joiner and author. His books included *The British Architect* (1745), *A Collection of Designs in Architecture* (1757), and *Designs in Carpentry* (1759).

Houghton Hall, Norfolk (1733); Edgcote House, Oxon (c.1750); Blair Castle, Perth and Kinross (1757, front staircase); and Kedleston Hall, Derbys (c.1759).

TALMAN, WILLIAM (1650–1719). Gentleman architect and interior designer. Pupil of Sir Christopher Wren. Comptroller of the Works, 1769–02.

South and east front of Chatsworth House, Derbys (1687–96); interior of Burghley House, Lincs (c.1688–90); Uppark, Sussex (c.1690); the east front of Dyrham Park, Glos (1698–1704); state apartments and gardens, Hampton Court Palace, London (1699–1702); Fetcham Park, Surrey (1700); stables at Wilton Hall, Bucks (1690s); Swallowfield Park, Berks (c.1690); and the south front of Drayton House, Northants (1702). Contributed to the design of Easton Neston, Northants (c.1695–1702).

TAYLOR, SIR ROBERT (1714–88). Neo-classical architect. Architect to the Office of Works. Trained as a stonemason, travelled to Italy (1740s), then about 1750 switched to architecture, in which he had immediate success. In the period between Burlington and Adam, he and James Paine were said to have divided the architectural practice of England between them.

Asgill House, Richmond, Surrey (1761–4); Danson House, Bexleyheath, Kent (c.1762–7); Purbrook House, Hants (1770, demolished 1837); Heveningham Hall, Suffolk (1778–c.1780, completed by James Wyatt in the nineteenth century); Gorhambury House, Herts (1777–90); and Sharpham House, Devon (c.1770).

THORNHILL, SIR JAMES (1675–1734). Decorative painter and part-time architect. Born at Thornhill Park, Dorset, the family house which he bought back.

Chatsworth House, Derbys (c.1702–8, west entrance hall, library ante-room, Sabine room, west front staircase, Yellow Silk drawing room); Easton Neston, Northants (1702–13, hall and staircase); Hanbury Hall, Worcs

(1710, hall, drawing room, staircase and bedchamber); Hampton Court Palace, London (before 1715, Queen's drawing room, closet and bedchamber, chapel and staircase); Cannons, London (1715–25, staircase, destroyed 1747); Gosfield Hall, Essex (after 1715, saloon); Sherborne House, Dorset (c.1715–20, staircase hall, staircase); Blenheim Palace, Oxon (1716, hall, saloon); Wimpole Hall, Cambs (1721–4); and Grimsthorpe Castle, Lincs (after 1722, hall, staircase). Many commissions in London.

THORNTON, WILLIAM (1670–1721). Joiner. From York.
> Castle Howard, N. Yorks (c.1706–11, wainscoting), Wentworth Castle, S. Yorks (c.1714, wainscoting, flooring), and Beningbrough Hall, N. Yorks (1716).

THORPE, JOHN (c.1565–c.1655). Architect. Along with Inigo Jones perhaps one of the first professional architects. Little is known about his life, but he probably had a hand in designing the houses listed her.
> Kirby Hall, Northants (1590s, semi-ruinous); Charlton House, London (1607–12); Longford Castle, Wilts (1590s, later much altered by James Wyatt and Anthony Salvin); Condover Hall, Salop (1590s); Audley End, Essex (1582–1614); Aston Hall, Warwicks (1618–35); Dowsby Hall, Lincs (c.1610); and Somerhill, Kent (c.1610–13).

THORP, JOHN (*fl.* 1706–28). Marble cutter. From Bakewell, Derbys.
> Castle Howard, N. Yorks (1711–2), Knowsley Hall, Lancs (1721), and perhaps Bramham Park, W. Yorks (1727).

TOMPION, THOMAS (1639–1713). Clockmaker, 'the father of English clockmaking'. Probably worked as a blacksmith until 1664 when he was apprenticed to a London clockmaker. He is first mentioned in 1670, became a member of the Clockmakers' Company in 1671 and was Master from 1704. In 1711 he formed a partnership with George Graham, his equally famous pupil. When the Royal Observatory was established in 1676 Tompion was selected to create two clocks that were very accurate and needed to be wound only once a year. He made about 5,500 watches and 700 clocks during his career. His clocks may be seen in the British Museum, Victoria and Albert Museum, Buckingham Palace, London Museum and Guildhall Museum, all in London, and also at Levens Hall, Cumb.

TRADESCANT, JOHN, THE ELDER (c.1570–1638). Gardener, plant collector and traveller. Gardener to the first and second Earls of Salisbury (Hatfield House and Salisbury House, London). Gardener to the first Duke of Buckingham (1623–8), working on his gardens at New Hall,

Essex (perhaps rebuilt in the early sixteenth century) and Burley-on-the-Hill House, Rut, and travelling to Russia, the Levant, Algiers and the Low Countries. Keeper to His Majesty's Gardens at Oatlands Park, Surrey (early sixteenth century, demolished 1649). An enthusiastic collector, he introduced many plants which are now staples.

TRADESCANT, JOHN, THE YOUNGER (1608–62). Gardener and botanist. Continued his father's work, travelling to Virginia at least once. Head Gardener to Charles I and worked on gardens to The Queen's House, London. Bequeathed his library and collection to Elias Ashmole to form the basis of the Ashmolean Museum, Oxford.

VANBRUGH, SIR JOHN (1664–1726). Soldier (Earl of Huntingdon's regiment, 1686, c.1692–1702), political prisoner (The Bastille, 1688–93), playwright (*The Relapse* (1696), *The Provok'd Wife* (1697)), Baroque architect (from 1699, Comptroller of Her Majesty's Works, 1702–13), herald (Clarenceux King at Arms, 1704–14) and wit. Superseded Talman in designing Castle Howard, with the help of Hawksmoor.

Castle Howard, N. Yorks (1699–1726); Blenheim Palace, Oxon (1704–16, completed by Hawksmoor after Vanbrugh's breach with the Duchess of Marlborough); Kimbolton Castle, Cambs (c.1707–10); Kings Weston, near Bristol (c.1710–19); Vanbrugh Castle, London (from 1718); Lake Pavilions, Rotondo, and four other buildings which have been demolished, Stowe House, Bucks (1719–24); Seaton Delaval Hall, Northumb (1720–28); Lumley Castle, Durham (1722, entrance front and interior); and north front (1722–6) and forecourt (1729–30) of Grimsthorpe Castle, Lincs.

VASSALLI, FRANCESCO (*fl.* 1724–63). Stuccoist. From near Lugano. Little is known of his life.

Duncombe Park, N. Yorks (c.1715, with Artari); Ditchley Park, Oxon (1725, with Artari); Aske Hall, N. Yorks (1730, hall); Towneley Hall, Lancs (1730–1, great hall); Castle Howard, N. Yorks (1736–7, Temple of the Four Winds); Petworth House, Sussex (1753, White and Gold room); Hagley Hall, Worcs (1758, White hall, dining room); and Shugborough Hall, Staffs (1763).

VERRIO, ANTONIO (c.1639–1707). Decorative painter. Born at Lecce, Italy, came to England about 1672 and stayed until his death.

Euston Hall, Suffolk (c.1675, Verrio's ceilings destroyed by fire in 1902); Windsor Castle, Berks (before 1677, largely destroyed during Wyatville's redecoration); Burghley House, Lincs (1687–98, all principal rooms); Ham House, Surrey (before 1698); Chatsworth House, Derbys (1698, great stairs, state dining room, library); and Hampton Court Palace, London (1700–4, King's staircase, King's bedroom, Queen's drawing room).

VILE, William: see **COBB**, John.

VOYSEY, CHARLES FRANCIS ANNESLEY (1857–1941), Arts and Crafts architect and interior designer. Set up in practice 1882. His houses set a fashion for speculative builders. He received hardly any commissions after 1918.

Perrycroft, Herefs (1893–4); Broad Leys (1898) and Moor Crag (1898–1900), both Cumb; The Pastures, Rut (1901); and The Orchard, Chorley Wood, Herts (1899–1901, his own house).

VULLIAMY, LEWIS (1791–1871). Architect. Pupil of Robert Smirke and very eclectic Victorian revivalist.

Boothby Pagnell Hall, Lincs (1823, in the Tudor style); Sewardstone Manor House, Essex (1845); Chestal House, Glos (1848, Jacobethan); Shernfold Park, Sussex (1853); Bramshott Grange, Hants (1855); Alderley House, Glos (1859–63); and Westonbirt House, Glos (1863–70, Tudorbethan).

WARING AND GILLOW. Furniture makers. Firm formed by the amalgamation in 1903 of Gillows, of Lancaster and London, and Waring, of Liverpool. Gillows was one of the most successful eighteenth-century firms, founded by Robert Gillow (1704–72) and continued by his sons Richard (1734–1811) and Robert (1745–93). Gillows supplied furniture to Queen Victoria, to country houses (there are pieces by Gillow in the drawing room at Dyrham Park, Glos), and to luxury yachts and liners. John Waring arrived in Liverpool from Belfast in 1835 and established a cabinet-making business, which was expanded by his son Samuel, who furnished hotels and public buildings. The firm was absorbed by Maples and Co. in 1980.

WEBB, JOHN (1611–1722). Palladian architect. Pupil (and relative by marriage) of Inigo Jones and assistant to Wren in building St Paul's Cathedral. Many of his houses have been destroyed.

Corinthian portico and north front of The Vyne, Hants (1654–6); and Amesbury Abbey, Wilts (1659–61).

WEBB, PHILIP (1831–1915). Eclectic Arts and Crafts architect and designer, and founder member of the Society for the Protection of

Ancient Buildings (1877). Worked in the office of G. E. Street, 1852–9, where he met William Morris.

> The Red House, Bexleyheath, Kent (1859–60, designed for William Morris); Benfleet Hall, Surrey (1860); Smeaton Manor, N. Yorks (1876–79, much altered); Standen, Surrey (1891–94); and Clouds House, Wilts (1876–91).

WEDGEWOOD, JOSIAH (1730–95). Pottery designer, credited with industrialising the manufacture of pottery. His firm provided tablets and roundels in coloured jasper-ware to insert in furniture.

WILKES, JOHN (?1680–?1730s). Locksmith. One of the best known of seventeenth/eighteenth century locksmiths.

> His work may be seen at Arbury Hall, Warwicks (before 1733), Stoneleigh Abbey Warwicks (1720-26), Chicheley Hall, Bucks (c. 1720), and also at the Victoria and Albert Museum.

WILKINS, WILLIAM (1778–1839). Architect. Son of an architect and antiquarian, also called William Wilkins (1751–1815). Pioneer of the Greek Revival. Travelled in Greece, Asia Minor and Italy (1802–6).

> Osberton House, Notts, which had the first Doric portico in Britain (c.1805, since greatly altered) and Northington Grange, Hants (1804–9), both in the Greek Revival style; Dalmeny House, West Lothian (1814–7) and Dunmore House, Stirling (1820–2, now ruinous), where he succumbed to the Tudorbethan style. Much of his work was in Cambridge (Downing College, King's College entrance screen, Trinity College New Court) and London (St George's Hospital, National Gallery, University College).

WILTON, JOSEPH (1722–1803). Sculptor. Worked for George III, Robert Adam and leading architects of the day.

> Croome Court, Worcs (1766, gallery chimneypiece), and Syon House, London (c.1767, gallery bas-reliefs).

WILTON, WILLIAM (*fl.* 1722–65). Plasterer. Father of Joseph Wilton.

> Stanmer House, Sussex (1722, entrance hall); Linley Hall, Salop (1765); and Firle Place, Sussex (c.1750, library attributed).

WINDE, WILLIAM (c.1640–1722). Architect, military engineer, soldier and garden designer.

> Coombe Abbey, Warwicks (1682–8, rebuilt); Castle Bromwich Hall, W. Mid (1686–1703, rebuilt and designed the gardens). Work at: Dingley Hall, Northants (1684–8); Belton House, Lincs (1685–8); Cliveden House, Bucks

(1676–8, rebuilt following its destruction by fire in 1795) and Buckingham House, London (1702–5, repeatedly altered and rebuilt, now Buckingham Palace). Laid out the terraces at Powis Castle, Powys (c.1680).

WISE, HENRY (1653–1738). Royal Gardener to Queen Anne (1702) and George I (1714) and landscape planner to the first Duke of Marlborough. Strongly influenced by French and Dutch formal garden designs. Apprenticed to George London and later his partner. London and Wise worked together at Blenheim Palace, Oxon, where their work was destroyed by 'Capability' Brown, but later partly reinstated.

Melbourne Hall, Derbys (1704, the yew alley, at 290 feet, thought to be the longest in Europe) and Dyrham Park, Glos (only a fragment of their design remains).

WOOD, JOHN THE ELDER (1704–54). Palladian architect of Bath, Som. Also designed Prior Park near Bath (1735–48).

WOOD, JOHN THE YOUNGER (1728–81). Palladian architect. Continued the work of his father in Bath.

Buckland House, Oxon (1755–8), and Tregenna Castle, Cornwall (1773–4).

WOOSTON, JOHN (*fl.* 1738–40). Plasterer. From Northampton.

Lamport Hall, Northants (1738, music hall, library ceiling); Faston Neston, Northants (dining room), and Althorp House, Northants (c.1733, work in the entrance hall), both attributed.

WREN, SIR CHRISTOPHER (1632–1723). Architect. Did not design any private houses (his work was in the universities of Oxford and Cambridge, royal palaces, public buildings and churches) but his influence on architecture in general was immense.

WRIGHT, RICHARD (d. 1771), and **ELWICK, EDWARD** (1721–94). Cabinet makers and upholsterers. The partnership, the most prominent in Yorkshire, lasted from 1747–71, enjoying a dominance comparable to that achieved by Gillows in Lancashire.

Supplied furniture to: Nostell Priory, W. Yorks; Worksop Manor, Notts; Temple Newsam House; W. Yorks, Cannon Hall, S. Yorks (much altered); and Wentworth Woodhouse, S. Yorks.

WYATT, JAMES (1746–1813). Architect. Prolific Neo-classical and Gothic architect who designed and altered over one hundred country houses. Went to Italy 1762–8. Worked initially with his elder brother Samuel. Heaton Hall, Lancs (c.1772–8) was his first country house. Sprang to fame with The Pantheon, Oxford Street, London (1769–72, demolished; his brother John was one of the shareholders of this venture). Samuel and James ran separate practices from 1774. Many of Wyatt's country houses have been destroyed or demolished, but some of the surviving ones are listed here.

Aston Hall, Salop (1789–93); Castle Coole, Co. Fermanagh (1790–7); Lasborough Park, Glos (1794); Allestree Hall, Derbys (1795); Longford Castle, Wilts (1796); Dodington Park, Glos (1798–1813); Norris Castle, IoW (1799); Belvoir Castle, Leics (1801–13, altered); Wycombe Abbey, Bucks (c.1803–4); and Ashridge House, Herts (1802–13, completed by Sir Jeffry Wyatville).

WYATT, LEWIS (1777–1853). Architect. Trained with his uncle Samuel, and then with his uncle James, and set up in practice c.1805.

Tatton Park, Ches (1807–18, completed); Willey Hall, Salop (1813–15); Cranage Hall, Ches (1828–9); and Sherborne House, Glos (1829–34).

WYATT, SAMUEL (1737–1807). Neo-classical architect. Elder brother of James.

Doddington Hall, Lincs (1777–98); several estate buildings at Holkham Hall, Norfolk (1780–1807); Tatton Park, Ches (1785–91, completed by his nephew, Lewis); and major alterations to Shugborough Hall, Staffs (1790–8).

WYATVILLE, SIR JEFFRY (1766–1840). Architect. Born Wyatt, changed his name 1824. Apprenticed to his uncle Samuel (c.1784–c.1792), joined the office of his uncle James (1792–9), and then left to set up a partnership with John Armstrong (1799). When James died (1813) he became the most eminent member of the family.

Windsor Castle (1824–37, major alterations); Lypiatt Park, Glos (1809, major alterations); Ashridge House, Herts (1814–7, completion of); Claverton Manor, Som (c.1820); Chatsworth House, Derbys (1820–41, major additions to); Dinton House (now Philipps House), Wilts (1814–7); Lilleshall Hall, Salop (1826–30); and Golden Grove, Carms (1826–37).

ZUCCHI, ANTONIO PIETRO (1726–95). Painter. Born in Venice, died in Rome. Second husband of Angelica Kauffmann (1781). Came to England about 1766. Worked principally for Robert Adam and also provided designs for furniture and carpets for other craftsmen to execute.

CONSTRUCTION GLOSSARY

TIMBER FRAMING

BRACE. A diagonal member strengthening a frame.

BRESSUMER, BRASTSUMMER, BREST SUMMER. A beam spanning an opening and supporting a wall above.

COLLAR. A beam joining a pair of rafters at purlin height.

COMMON RAFTER. A rafter supported by a purlin

CROWN POST, CROWN PLATE. An alternative to purlins. Each pair of common rafters is joined by a collar resting upon a central crown plate. This is supported by crown posts, which in turn rest on the tie-beam.

CRUCK. A large curved timber rising from the ground to the ridge, forming at once wall timbers and a pair of principal rafters.

DRAGON BEAM. A horizontal floor beam in jettied buildings with two or more adjacent jetties. It runs from corner to corner so that the floor joists, which are tenoned into it, are always at right angles to the wall.

HAMMER BEAM, HAMMER POST. A means of increasing the width or height of a building. The tie-beam is cut through and the portions remaining, the hammerbeams, are supported by curved braces from the wall. The hammer beam supports a hammer post which in turn supports the collar.

JETTY. An upper wall which projects beyond the lower wall, forming an overhang.

KING POST. A central post rising from the tie beam or collar and supporting the roof ridge.

PRINCIPAL RAFTER. Rafter supporting a purlin.

PURLIN. A roof beam running the length of a building, carried on the principal rafters and supporting the common rafters.

QUEEN POST. A pair of posts rising from the tie beam and supporting the purlin.

SOLEPLATE. The horizontal member forming the base of a frame.

TIE-BEAM. A beam running the width of the building, tying together the feet of a pair of principal rafters.

WALLPLATE. The horizontal member forming the top of a frame.

WINDBRACE. A brace running from principal rafter to purlin, to stiffen the roof structure.

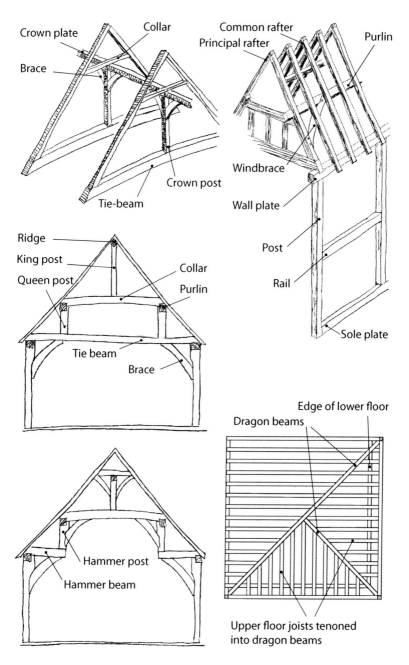

Crown plate · Collar
Brace
Crown post
Tie-beam

Common rafter · Principal rafter · Purlin
Windbrace
Wall plate
Post
Rail
Sole plate

Ridge
King post
Queen post
Collar
Purlin
Tie beam
Brace

Hammer post
Hammer beam

Edge of lower floor
Dragon beams
Upper floor joists tenoned
into dragon beams

The Country House Companion – 41

STONEWORK

ASHLAR. Dressed, rectangular stonework laid in courses and bonded.

COURSED RUBBLE. Roughly dressed, roughly coursed stone.

CYCLOPEAN, ROCK-FACED. Masonry of large, irregularly shaped stones.

KEYSTONE. A wedge-shaped stone at the centre of an arch, locking the structure.

QUOIN. The stones forming the corner of a building, often decorated so that they contrast with the walls.

RANDOM RUBBLE. Undressed stone, laid uncoursed.

RUBBLE. Stonework of undressed or roughly dressed stones.

RUSTICATED. Stone cut with joints exaggerated and the surface projecting beyond the joints. The surface can be plain, but is usually textured or decorated.

SQUARED RUBBLE. Stones roughly cut square or rectangular.

BRICKWORK

BONDING. Bricks laid with the joints between them overlapping.

DIAPER BONDING. Bricks of different colours laid to create a pattern.

ENGLISH BOND. Bricks in alternate courses of headers and stretchers.

FLEMISH BOND. Alternate headers and stretchers in each course.

HEADER. Brick laid so that its shortest face is exposed.

HEADER BOND. Bricks laid with only their headers showing.

ON EDGE. Brick laid on the shortest side.

SOLDIER. Brick laid on end.

STRETCHER. Brick laid so that its longest face is exposed.

STRETCHER BOND. Bricks laid with only their stretchers showing.

DOORS

CASEMENT or SASH DOOR. A door glazed above the middle rail.

DOUBLE MARGIN DOOR. A door with the muntin twice as wide as usual and finished in the same manner as the stiles, thus appearing to be a double door.

DUTCH, STABLE or **HALF DOOR.** A door divided into two halves horizontally, so that the bottom half can remain shut when the top half is opened.

FALSE or **SHAM DOOR.** Imitation door.

FLUSH DOOR. A door with its back and front finished quite plain (usually with plywood).

FOLDING DOOR. A door divided vertically into two or more parts, hinged to each other.

FRAMED DOOR. A door with a timber frame all round.

FRAMED, LEDGED, BRACED AND BATTENED. A door which is framed all round (framed), with horizontal members at the top, middle and bottom (ledged), and two diagonal members (braced). It is covered on the outside with boards (battens). Common varients are ledged and battened, and ledged, braced and battened.

JIB DOOR. Flush door meant to look like part of the wall.

MIDDLE or **LOCK RAIL.** A horizontal rail in the middle to which the lock is fitted.

MUNTIN. The vertical central member in a framed door.

PANELLED DOOR. A framed door in which the stiles, muntin and rails are exposed and probably decorated, and the spaces between them are filled with panels.

RAIL. Horizontal members of a framed door.

STILES. The vertical members on each side of most types of door.

WICKET. A small door cut into a large one.

WINDOWS

BAY WINDOW. A window projecting from a wall.

BOW WINDOW. A curved window projecting from a wall.

DORMER WINDOW. A window projecting from the roof. (Strictly, built on the rafters. A roof window which continues the line of the wall is a lucarne).

CASEMENT WINDOW. A window light hung with hinges at one of its sides.

DIOCLETIAN or **THERMAL WINDOW.** A semicircular window divided into three by two plain mullions.

FRENCH WINDOW. A glazed pair of doors, normally opening outwards.

LANCET WINDOW. Originally, an Early English window, narrow and with a steeply pointed arch, either placed singly or in groups.

LATTICE WINDOW. Any window made up of small lozenge-shaped panes of glass.

LIGHT or **SASH.** Fixed or opening glazed frame, one or more forming a window.

MULLION. A bar dividing a window vertically.

ORIEL WINDOW. Bay window on an upper storey.

PALLADIAN, VENETIAN or **SERLIANA WINDOW.** Tripartite window, the central part with a semicircular arch over it. The three parts were commonly divided by columns or pilasters.

SASH. Properly, 'sliding sash' or 'hung sash', the 'sash' being a synonym for 'light'. A window with two lights, one above the other, one or both of which moves vertically by means of a cord with a counterweight attached to each side. Invented in England (or possibly the Netherlands) in the 1670s.

TRANSOM. A bar dividing a window horizontally.

WINDOW GLASS. Manufactured from the fifteenth century. 'Crown glass' was made by blowing a large bubble of glass, cutting open the top, and spinning the glass into a large disc. This was cut into small diamonds (later into small rectangles) which were set in lead frames. For 'broad glass', the bubble was worked into a cylinder which was cut down its length, producing a flat sheet about a foot wide and five feet long. Window glass, cheaply manufactured in large sheets, appeared around 1830.

WYATT WINDOW. Similar to a Palladian window, but without the arch over the central part. Named after James Wyatt.

STAIRCASES

After the Middle Ages, the staircase quickly changed from being simply a means of climbing from one floor to another to a means of making a grandiose architectural statement about taste, wealth and learning. This is the case in almost every country house built since that time.

_____

BALUSTERS, BANISTERS. Short posts supporting the handrail.

TURNED BALUSTERS are turned (i.e. circular in section) on a lathe.

VASE-SHAPED BALUSTERS are turned balusters in the shape of a vase.

TWISTED BALUSTERS are turned balusters in a twisted or spiral shape.

MIXED BALUSTERS are of different turned shapes.

SPLAT BALUSTERS are formed from flat planks of wood.

BALUSTRADE. The balusters together with the handrail.

BULLNOSE. The bottom step, when this is wider than the rest. The tread is often rounded at one or both ends.

CAP. See **NEWEL**.

CIRCULAR STAIR. Staircase curving round a open stairwell.

DOG-LEG. Staircase with a half-space landing.

DROP. See **NEWEL**.

EASING. Shaped junction between strings when the staircase changes direction.

FLIGHT. Straight series of steps between landings, or between floors, or between floor and landing.

FLYING STAIRCASE. Staircase in which the treads are cantilevered out from the stairwell walls and there is no newel at the corners.

GEOMETRICAL STAIRCASE. Circular or oval flying staircase.

HALF-TURN STAIR. Staircase which is split by quarter-landings.

LANDING. A small level space between flights.

HALF-SPACE, HALF-LANDING: landing which is the width of two parallel flights, one ascending and one descending.

QUARTER-SPACE, QUARTER-LANDING: landing which connects two flights at ninety degrees to each other.

NEWEL. (1) The top or bottom post supporting a handrail. The top part of it is called the CAP and the bottom part the DROP. (2) The central post of a spiral staircase.

NOSING. Front edge of a tread, projecting over the riser and usually rounded.

RISER. The vertical section between treads.

OPEN RISER. staircase with no risers.

SERVICE STAIR. Secondary staircase used by servants.

SPIRAL STAIR. Circular staircase set around a central newel.

STAIR TURRET, VICE. Narrow tower housing a spiral staircase.

STRING. Vertical board covering the ends of the treads and risers.

  OPEN STRING STAIR. One with no string.

TREAD. The top surface of the step, the part that is trodden upon.

VICE. See **STAIR TURRET**.

VOLUTE. The spiral-shaped handrail when the staircase starts with a bullnose.

WELL STAIR. Staircase rising by short straight flights along the sides of a square or rectangular well.

WINDER. A tread which is wider at one end than the other, used when a staircase makes a turn without a landing.

  KITE WINDER. The middle of three winders when the staircase makes a ninety degree turn.

FIREPLACES, CHIMNEYPIECES AND CHIMNEYS

Like the staircase, the fireplace rose from humble beginnings to architectural heights. Before the late fifteenth century, the fire was in the middle of the great hall and the smoke escaped as best it might. In the largest houses, cooking was done elsewhere, although in smaller ones, the fire served for both heating and cooking.

In the sixteenth century, the fireplace, often still immensely large, moved from a central position to a side position, against an outside wall. The smoke was gathered by a chimney hood, and chimneys, often built on rather than integrated into the wall, became common, although very expensive. Country house owners drew attention to the number of fireplaces they had, and so to their wealth, by making the chimneys prominent and very elaborate.

A horizontal board, the overmantel, was often placed above the fire to improve heat circulation. In the seventeenth century, the fireplace, the overmantel and the space above the overmantel tended to become one architectural unit, often magnificent and dominating the room, with decorative panels, busts, mirrors or carvings above the fireplace. With the advent of the Palladian and Neo-classical styles in the eighteenth century, fireplaces became taller and shallower, and chimneys longer, to improve the draught. This interrupted the pure, 'flat' roofline so chimneys were then hidden, or mostly hidden, by parapets, or grouped in one place (e.g. end-stacked). The same is true of classical revival country houses of the nineteenth and earlier twentieth centuries. With the increasing use of coal rather than wood, fireplaces became smaller; in the case of older fireplaces, sometimes with the help of an insert.

UTILITIES

Although most basic utilities had an early beginning, they were exceptionally slow to take root in the country house. The water closet, for example, was in use in the sixteenth century, but only came into common use in the late nineteenth century. a group of outside toilets (using ash to cover poo)

Other utilities, such as gas, electricity and central heating, had to wait to be discovered. But even so, their adoption by the country house was painfully slow.

PLUMBING

As with most items of plumbing, the country house lagged well behind the rest of the field in the provision of running water. Those country houses which were based on religious foundations (after the Dissolution of the Monasteries, 1536–41) were luckier than most, since monasteries were invariably situated where there was a good source of water. Throughout the sixteenth century, houses on hilltops or slopes had to rely on wells, or rainwater run-off collected in cisterns. By 1700 the hand-pump had been introduced, but it could only raise water some fifteen feet. The water-wheel was introduced at about the same time, capable of raising water up to one hundred feet, but this only became common in the second half of the seventeenth century: water wheels were installed at Uppark, Sussex, Euston Hall, Suffolk, Broadlands, Hants, and Blenheim Palace, Oxon. The steam engine was introduced in the early eighteenth century, but there is no evidence for its extensive use. Witley Court (Worcs) employed one.

Piped hot water was heated by a boiler (sometimes central, sometimes in individual bathrooms) with a water tank above it.

Water closets became common around 1830 and wash basins around 1860. The latter were initially placed near the entrance hall and by the smoking and billiard rooms.

Modern baths were slow to take off: some were evident by 1870 but many country houses had none. The preferred method before baths and bathrooms became common was to use a hip bath set up in front of the fire in the bedroom.

HEATING

Three central heating systems were developed around 1800: steam, hot air and hot water. Steam heating, by means of steam travelling through steam pipes, was expensive and not very effective, although it was installed at Sir Walter Scott's house at Abbotsford, Borders, in 1823. It died out quite quickly. Hot air, by means of hot air travelling through ducts, was an early favourite. It was installed at Coleshill, Berks, in 1814 and Osmaston Manor, Derbys, in 1846–9 (both demolished). Hot water, passed through pipes and radiators, was ultimately the favourite. It was installed at Stratfield Saye, Hants, for the Duke of Wellington in 1833 and Mentmore Towers, Bucks, in 1850–5.

Used of course by the Romans for under floor heating.

For some time, central heating did not include the whole house, only the entrance hall, the main reception room downstairs, and perhaps the corridors. Nor was it universally approved: as late as 1880 J. J. Stevenson in his well-regarded book *House Architecture* wrote: 'the best system, on the whole, is the old one of open fires.'

At Witley Court (Worcs) the Earl of Dudley (Ward) who owned many coal mines and so was able to get large supplies delivered — had coal fired heating as well as open fires.

LIGHTING

Gas lighting, which appeared around the turn of the eighteenth and nineteenth centuries (Sir Walter Scott installed it at Abbotsford, Borders, in 1823), had several disadvantages. One was the smell; another was the heat given off; and the third was the great amount of gas need to provide only a moderate light. About 1885 the gas mantle was invented, which was more economical and gave off less heat. To light a whole country house, however, involved either building a private gasworks (as at Tyntesfield, Som), or linking up to the public

Pongy coal gas.

gasworks (as at Stanmore Hall, Salop, which drew its gas from the municipal gasworks at Bridgnorth).

Gas lighting began to be replaced by electricity towards the end of the nineteenth century. Cragside, Northumb, was the first country house in the United Kingdom to have electric lighting installed (1880). Others soon followed, including Hatfield House, Herts (1880–1), Stokesay Court, Salop (1889) and Tyntesfield, Som (1890). The earliest country house where electricity for lighting was part of the construction was Smallwood Manor, Staffs (1886).

Some houses as in all other mod. cons lagged behind still using candles or oil lamps (eg. Calke Abbey Staffs)

NAMES AND FUNCTIONS OF ROOMS

In the mediaeval period, there were only two main rooms in the larger houses, the great hall and the solar, both of which served many different functions. Subsequently, the use of space became more specialized and many more rooms, each with a specific purpose, were added. This process reached its apogee in the mid-nineteenth century when breakfast rooms (and even luncheon rooms), morning rooms, smoking rooms, gun rooms, billiard rooms and nurseries were brought into use. Unfortunately, nearly all surviving Victorian country houses have been converted into schools, colleges, hotels, conference centres or apartments, and the original layout of the rooms has been obscured (see Mark Girouard's *The Victorian Country House* for the original plans of many houses). Tyntesfield, Som, is one example where the elaborate room structure of the 1860s is still preserved.

BAKEHOUSE. For preparing and baking bread, biscuits and cakes. The bakehouse disappeared after commercial bakeries arrived.
Charlecote Park, Warwicks (eighteenth century); Erddig Hall, Denbighshire (eighteenth century); Prestwold Hall, Leics (1842–4); and Lanhydrock, Cornwall (after 1881).

BANQUETING HALL Originally, a room to retire to after the meal, to enjoy a dessert of wafers and spices ('banquet'). Later, a building separate from the main house, in which meals would be taken.

Lacock Abbey, Wilts (c.1550); Longleat House, Wilts (1568–9); Montacute House, Som (1590s); Camden House, Glos (c.1610, house destroyed but the two banqueting houses survive); The Dog Kennel, Chatelherault, Lanarkshire (c.1730); Bowling Green House, Wrest Park, Beds (c.1740); Carné's Seat, Goodwood House, Sussex (c.1743); The Menagerie, Northants (1750s); The Banqueting House, Gibside, Tyne & W. (1751, house ruined but banqueting hall intact); and The Pineapple, Dunmore Park, Stirling (1761).

BATHROOM. Bathrooms in private houses were slow to develop and for some centuries were the preserve of the very wealthy; even kings bathed in wooden tubs. A bathroom with taps was installed at Chatsworth House, Derbys, in 1697, and at Carshalton House, Surrey (1719–20), both worthy of public comment at the time. Bathing became fashionable in the eighteenth century and some houses had a bathhouse in the grounds. Gradually baths were introduced inside, but most country houses before 1880 had only one bathroom, for family use. It was only by 1900 that bathrooms became relatively common.

BEDROOM, BEDCHAMBER. The concept of a bedchamber, used primarily for sleeping, became common in the mid-sixteenth century. Thereafter it varied in importance: in the late seventeenth century it was used for receiving visitors; in the eighteenth century and thereafter it became smaller and more private.

BILLIARD ROOM. The first billiard room was built at Southill Park, Beds, sometime between 1767 and 1803, and more than two-thirds of country houses built between 1835 and 1870 had a billiard room. This commonly adjoined the smoking room: smoking and billiards were almost exclusively male pastimes.

Tyntesfield, Som (1863); Lanhydrock, Cornwall (1881); Eastnor Castle, Herefs (1810–20, the Little Library); and Cragside, Northumb (1870–85).

BOUDOIR. A room off her bedroom or dressing room in which the lady of the house could be private and receive friends.

BREAKFAST ROOM, BREAKFAST PARLOUR. Appears to have been invented in the early nineteenth century. Before that, breakfast was presumably eaten in the dining room.

Calke Abbey, Derbys (mid-nineteenth century).

BREWHOUSE. For brewing beer. Beer was drunk at all times, including breakfast, in the days before safe drinking water.

Lacock Abbey, Wilts (mid-sixteenth century); Shugborough Hall, Staffs (eighteenth century); and Charlecote Park, Warwicks (eighteenth century).

BRUSHING ROOM. For brushing clothes which could not be washed. Originally, a small room off the main bedchambers. By the beginning of the nineteenth century brushing was done, at specified times, in the servants' hall, and fifty years later the brushing room was included in the outside service rooms.

Standen, Sussex (1891–4) and Ken Hill, Norfolk (1879–80).

BUTTERY. Where casks of beer and other drinks were stored while they were being served.

CABINET. See **CLOSET**.

CHAPEL. Common in houses before the mid-seventeenth century, thereafter only in larger houses. *(Some R.C. ones survive - hidden before they were permitted in the late 18c)*

Belton House, Lincs (1680s); Wimpole Hall, Cambs (1719–21); Holkham Hall, Norfolk (mid-eighteenth century); and Ashridge House, Herts (1808–13). *Chatsworth House (Derbys). R.C at Spetchley Park (Worcs)*

CLOSET, CABINET. Small private room adjacent to the bedroom. The close stool (chamber pot) was often kept there.

Queen's closet, Ham House, Surrey (late seventeenth century).

DAIRY. For producing cream, butter and cheese. Usually on the north side of the house (for coolness).

Georgian dairy, Berrington Hall, Herefs (1778–81).

DINING ROOM. Until about 1800, normally called the eating room (*salle á manger*). In the eighteenth century, this replaced the great chamber as a place for formal eating and increasingly became a place for show and display.

Danson House, Kent (1760s); Goodwood House, Sussex (1802); Scampston Hall, N. Yorks (c.1820); Cragside, Northumb (1870–2); and Tyntesfield, Som (c.1885).

DRAWING ROOM. In the late sixteenth and early seventeenth centuries, simply a private sitting room. In the eighteenth century and after, it was regarded as a feminine room to which the women withdrew while the men smoked and drank after dinner. *[withdrawing room]*

Wimpole Hall, Cambs (1791); Shugborough Hall, Staffs (1794); and Brodsworth Hall, S. Yorks (1861–70).

DRESSING ROOM. In the second half of the seventeenth century some houses had dressing rooms for husband and wife attached to their common bedroom. In the eighteenth century, a lady dressed in the bedroom; later on in her boudoir.

Houghton Hall, Norfolk (1726–31) and Holkham Hall, Norfolk (1734–62).

GALLERIES. A room dedicated to the display of objects became popular in the eighteenth century as a result of the Grand Tour. Previously, the long gallery had frequently housed pictures and sculptures. See also LONG GALLERY. The Elizabethan invention for indoor promenading & exercise especially in inclement weather..

Picture galleries: Hardwick Hall, Derbys, (1590–6); Corsham Court, Wilts ('Capability' Brown, 1760s); Attingham Park, Salop (for Lord Berwick, 1805); and Petworth House, Sussex (for Lord Egremont, 1830s). Sculpture galleries: Chiswick House, London (for Lord Burlington, 1724); Holkham Hall, Norfolk (1734); Newby Hall, N. Yorks (1760s); and Chatsworth House, Derbys (1825). Aston Hall (West Mids), Little Moreton Hall (Cheshire) both traditional long galleries.

GARDEROBE. Lavatory which discharged either on to bare earth or direct into the moat.

GREAT CHAMBER, SOLAR. An upper chamber, reached by stairs from the hall, where the owner could receive guests, dine and sleep.

Cothay Manor, Som (late fifteenth century); Great Chalfield Manor, Wilts (c.1475); Gilling Castle, N. Yorks (1585); Hardwick Hall, Derbys (1597); and Chastleton House, Oxon (c.1614).

GUN ROOM. Room for keeping guns and, by association, for the joviality following a shoot. Introduced about 1870.

Cragside, Northumb (1869–84) and St Alban's Court, Kent (1875–8).

HALL. In early country houses, the biggest and largest room. At one end was the dais at which the owner and his friends sat while dining. At the other were the screens, creating a passage, from which the kitchen was reached. By the seventeenth century, the hall had become the entrance feature rather than a living room. Later still (nineteenth century), it once more became a communal room.

Penshurst Place, Kent (early fourteenth century); Rufford Old Hall, Lancs (early sixteenth century); Blenheim Palace, Oxon (c.1719); Ashridge House, Herts (1808); Canford Manor, Dorset (mid-nineteenth century); and Wightwick Manor, W. Mid (1893). Aston Hall (early 17c) West Midlands

KITCHEN. In early country houses, housed in a separate building (to reduce the fire risk). It moved to the main house in the Tudor period, surrounded by other service rooms, either round a courtyard or on the far side of the hall screens from the hall. Typical facilities of this period were an open range and a brick-built stove, burning charcoal. In the eighteenth century, it was common for the kitchen and other service rooms to be placed in a separate pavilion or wing. The enclosed cast iron stove was introduced in the nineteenth century, doing away with the brick-built stove and, to some extent, with the open hearth, along with an increasingly extensive range of cooking utensils.

Stanton Harcourt Manor, Oxon (Mediaeval); Burghley House, Lincs (late sixteenth century); Holkham Hall, Norfolk (1757); Charlecote Park, Warwicks (mid-nineteenth century); and Lanhydrock, Cornwall (1880s).

LARDER. Originally, a store for raw meat. This later became the wet larder. The dry larder was for storing everything else, although many houses had a fish larder, bacon larder and game larder.

LAUNDRY. Washing was a continuous process in all but the smallest country houses. The wash house or wet laundry was equipped with a large copper or coppers, washing troughs, and a pump to bring in water. There was also a drying loft or closet, and a dry laundry room for pressing and ironing.

Erddig Hall, Den (eighteenth century?); Charlecote Park, Warwicks (eighteenth century); Shugborough Hall, Staffs (c.1800); Pakenham Hall, Co. Westmeath (early nineteenth century; now Tullynally Castle); Berrington Hall, Herefs (mid-nineteenth century); Castle Ward, Co. Down (mid-nineteenth century); and Beningbrough Hall, N. Yorks (mid-nineteenth century).

LIBRARY. In the seventeenth century and earlier, books were usually housed in a cabinet close to the bedchamber, or in a closet. The library as a separate room only became common in the eighteenth century. Over 2,200 country house libraries are known from this period. The family used the library not only as a place to write and read, but also as a living room. Libraries were at their most magnificent in the late eighteenth and early nineteenth century and declined in popularity thereafter. Many were subsequently split up or sold off to meet debts and, later on, death duties. Forty thousand volumes of the Grenville library at Stowe House, Bucks were sold in 1840. Other libraries disposed of in this way include those from Althorp, Northants, Blenheim Palace, Oxon and Castle Howard, N. Yorks.

Holkham Hall, Norfolk (c.1745); Althorp House, Northants (1819); Tatton Park, Ches (c.1810); and Sheringham Hall, Norfolk (1812–9).

Some libraries were used, but often books could be bought by the yard for the appearance.

LONG GALLERY. A long, narrow room full of windows on at least two sides, used for indoor sport, some outdoor sports when it was wet, a picture gallery, conversation and perambulation. Long galleries were built from about 1550 to 1650. Many were later converted to libraries or picture galleries. See also **GALLERIES.**

The Vyne, Hants (1520s); Haddon Hall, Derbys (c.1550, altered 1603); Little Moreton Hall, Ches (1580s); Hardwick Hall, Derbys (1597); Knole Park, Kent (c.1610); and Blickling Hall, Norfolk (c.1620). *Aston Hall West Midlands* *Little Moreton Hall Cheshire*

MORNING ROOM. Appeared in the early nineteenth century and disappeared about a hundred years later. An informal sitting room, mostly for ladies.

Harlaxton Manor, Lincs (1832–44); Horsted Place, Sussex (1850–1); and Standen, Sussex (1891–4).

MUSIC ROOM. Became common after about 1750, sometimes with an organ installed.

Kedleston Hall, Derbys (c.1760); Newby Hall, N. Yorks (c.1765); Killerton House, Devon (c.1800); Shadwell Park, Norfolk (1840–3 and 1855–60); Highclere Castle, Hants (1840–50); and Kelham Hall, Notts (1858–61).

NURSERY. Before purpose-designed nurseries were built in the early nineteenth century, children spent their early years on the attic floor in whatever room was convenient. In the Victorian period, the family often lived in self-contained quarters. The nursery was usually located on the floor above the adult rooms, and might have comprised a day nursery (a living and eating room), a night nursery (a bedroom), accommodation for the governess or nanny, and a school room.

Nunnington Hall, N. Yorks (restored 1920s); Lanhydrock, Cornwall (1880s); and Dalemain, Cumb (nineteenth century).

PARLOUR. In the days of the great hall, the parlour was a small room for the family to dine in, sometimes doubling up as a bedchamber. In later usage it was simply a sitting room.

Haddon Hall, Derbys (thirteenth century) and, at the other extreme, Wightwick Manor, W. Mid (1887–93).

PANTRY. Where bread and grain were kept and, later on, dairy products and some cooked dishes.

PASTRY. Where pastries and meat pies were made and, in the nineteenth century, sweets, tarts and confectionery.

SALOON. From the late seventeenth century, a grand reception room leading off the hall, serving as a replacement for the great chamber. It became a showcase for the best pictures, sculptures and pieces of furniture.

Ragley Hall, Warwicks (1678); Blenheim Palace, Oxon (1705–22); Hagley Hall, Warwicks (c.1750); Holkham Hall, Norfolk (mid-eighteenth century); Saltram, Devon (1768); and Belvoir Castle, Rut (mid-nineteenth century).

SCULLERY. Room where washing-up was done and such jobs as chopping and washing vegetables, preparing meat and gutting fish.

Lanhydrock, Cornwall (1880s) and Charlecote Park, Warwicks (nineteenth century).

SERVANTS' HALL. From the late seventeenth century, a large room for the servants to meet, sit and dine communally. The housekeeper's and butler's room often adjoined it. Sometimes there was discrimination: at Longleat House, Wilts, for example, the senior servants (head butler, cook, ladies' maids, valets, grooms of the chamber) would eat in the steward's room while the lower staff ate in the servants' hall.

Erddig Hall, Den (1684–7); Peckforton Castle, Ches (1844–50); and Standen, Sussex (1892–4).

SERVANTS' BARRACKS. From the late seventeenth century, dormitory for servants, normally in the attics but often in the basement or (for men) in the stables or outhouses.

Mamhead Park, Devon (early 1830s).

SMOKING ROOM. A room introduced in the mid-nineteenth century usually adjoining the billiard room. Previously men had smoked in the servants hall, in the kitchen, outdoors or in the stables.

Shadwell Park, Norfolk (1840–2, 1856–60) and Highclere Castle, Hants (1840–50).

SOLAR. See **GREAT CHAMBER.**

STATE BEDROOM. Reserved for the sovereign or guests of superior rank to the host.

Hardwick Hall, Derbys (1590s); Holkham Hall, Norfolk (1734–62); Houghton Hall, Norfolk (1726–31); Kedleston Hall, Derbys (c.1758); Powis Castle, Powys (late seventeenth century); Chatsworth House, Derbys (late seventeenth century); and Waddesdon Manor, Bucks (1874–89).

STILLROOM. Originally, in the sixteenth century, the room where the stills (distillers) were kept for the production of perfumes, medicines and cordial waters. Later (late seventeenth century) polishes, waxes and soaps would be made, until the eighteenth century when it became cheaper to buy them. In the nineteenth century the stillroom was used for making preserves, pickles and desserts.

WITHDRAWING ROOM. See DRAWING ROOM.

FLOOR COVERINGS AND CARPETS

In early houses, the floors were covered with rushes or straw, and strewn with herbs and sweet-smelling flowers in summer. By the late sixteenth century, rush and straw mats were laid down. These were sold to the larger houses in rolls: an eighty-yard roll bought in 1611 cost 13s 4d, about £1,300 today. There were carpets at this time, but they were used as furniture coverings, placed over tables, trunks and cupboards, but rarely on the floor. The best furniture carpets came from Turkey and Persia, the former giving rise to an English imitation style known as turkey work.

In the seventeenth century, carpets (sometimes of leather) began to be placed on floors and this became the norm in eighteenth century houses. Pile carpets, with such famous names as Wilton and Axminster, were available from the 1740s onwards. These were restricted in use to the main rooms and, right up until the end of the nineteenth century, were taken up every summer. Such carpets could be made to order to fit a particular room. A large customised Axminster carpet cost £100 in 1778 (£136,000 today). For areas of lesser importance in the house, such as passages and servants' quarters, painted floor cloths of canvas and oil paint were used, and from 1863 onwards linoleum.

WALL COVERINGS

It was not until the late twentieth century that people were content to cover their bare walls with a plain coat of magnolia emulsion. For many centuries before, bare walls had needed disguising. From the very earliest years, tapestry ('arras') was the answer or, for the less rich, painted cloth. Later, panelling and leather hangings came in; later still, damask and stucco. In spite of its early introduction, wallpaper was the last to win popularity.

DAMASK. A reversible patterned fabric, usually woven from silk but sometimes wool, used as a wall covering in the eighteenth century. It was at this time that hanging pictures became fashionable (and houses were made lighter with more windows) so wall coverings that displayed them to best advantage were required. Damask was a favourite; it was stretched across battens and fixed permanently in place.

LEATHER. Embossed leather wall hangings made in panels were popular in the United Kingdom from 1600–1740 . They originated in North Africa, arriving in Spain in the ninth century and in Flanders from the fourteenth, where manufacturing was centred on Mechelen. The wet leather was stretched over a wooden mould and, when dry, was painted, gilded and lacquered. Sometimes sheets of silver foil were glued on following a design drawn from a cartoon. The highlights were then hand-tooled and the sheets covered with oil paint and glazes to allow the burnished metal to shine through.

Levens Hall, Cumb (1590s), and the East Hall at Dyrham Park, Glos (1692–1704, covered with Dutch embossed leather).

PAINTED CLOTH. For those who could not afford tapestries, painted cloth offered a cheaper alternative from the fifteenth to the seventeenth centuries. The designs were painted on hempen cloth or osnaburg. Few have survived. Painted cloth was superseded in the eighteenth century by Indian textiles and then printed European ones.

Queen's room, Belton House, Lincs (1684, design on canvas survives)

PANELLING. Sixteenth and seventeenth centuries. Wooden wall covering of flat panels with dividers. The panels might be decorated, for example with strapwork or linenfold.

STUCCO. Interior and exterior wall finish, known from antiquity, made of lime, sand and water. It was a component of lath and plaster wall finishes, in which thin wooden strips supported the stucco, and was also widely used as a sculptural material.

TAPESTRIES. Large country houses required a great deal of tapestry to adorn their walls (160 yards-worth for Hengrave Hall, Suffolk, in 1603). The main centre for the manufacture of tapestry in the fourteenth, fifteenth and sixteenth centuries was the Low Countries: Arras, Bruges, Brussels and Tournai. The earliest surviving British tapestry was made in 1588 by Richard Hicks at William Sheldon's works and is now in the Victoria and Albert Museum. Subsequently, they were produced in 'factories' such as those established in 1620 at Mortlake Tapestry Works in London (which for a time produced some of the finest tapestries in Europe; it closed in 1771) and Les Gobelins in Paris. The designs were often produced by painters. Biblical and mythological scenes were common. 'Verdure' tapestries showed trees and flowers. 'Soho' tapestries (late sixteenth and early seventeenth centuries) were more exotic and in demand for their Indian subjects and their chinoiserie. By this time, entire rooms could be completely decorated with tapestries. Tapestries went out of fashion at the end of the eighteenth century, but returned in the 1880s, as part of the Arts and Crafts movement. William Morris founded the Merton Abbey works in 1881.

> Tapestry rooms at: Osterley Park, London (1761); and Belton House, Lincs (1684)). Tapestries at: Burghley House, Lincs (1558–87); Hardwick Hall, Derbys (begun 1590); Blenheim Palace, Oxon (1705–19); and Houghton Hall, Norfolk (1722–35).

WALLPAPER. Wallpaper dates from as early as 1509 in the United Kingdom (at Christ's College, Cambridge) but only really established itself in the early eighteenth century due to manufacturing improvements. At about the same time Chinese hand-painted wallpaper was imported from the Far East. Both were produced in rolls. A fresh impetus was added between 1864 and 1876 when William Morris produced his first wallpaper designs; they are still in use today.

FURNISHING FABRICS

ATLAS. A glossy satin or silk fabric.

BAIZE. Lightweight woollen fabric similar to flannel.

BROADCLOTH. An English wool woven on a broad loom. Waterproof and used mainly for outdoor clothes but also to cover furniture.

BROCADE. Heavy silk fabric, with slightly raised patterns.

BUCKRAM. Cheap, loose woven cloth used as a lining.

CAFFOY. A wool fabric in imitation of silk damasks.

CALAMANCO. Worsted material, chequered on one side only, used for hangings and upholstery.

CALICO. Fabric made of cotton, or cotton and linen. Used for dresses and hangings.

CANVAS. Cotton or linen fabric, varying from fine to coarse.

CHINTZ. Painted or printed cloths, originally from India. Popular in the eighteenth century for window curtains, wall and bed hangings, and furniture upholstery.

CRETONNE. Stout cotton fabric which supplanted chintz for furniture upholstery.

CREWEL. Embroidery yarn in use from the seventeenth century onwards.

DAMASK. Reversible fabric, woven from silk (for petticoats and dresses), wool (upholstery), or linen (for table linen).

DARNIX, DORNICK. Silk, worsted or woollen fabric used for hangings, carpets and household linen.

DIAPER. Cotton or linen fabric with diagonal pattern of lozenges, used for household linen.

DIMITY. Strong cotton fabric, sometimes with patterned stripes, used for bedroom hangings.

DOILY. Originally a fringed napkin. In the nineteenth century referred to any round linen or cotton mat placed on plates under cakes etc.

DRUGGET. Originally a cheap cloth of wool, or wool and silk, used for outer clothes; subsequently a protective cloth placed over carpets. Also used in upholstery.

DURANT. Hard-wearing wool sometimes used as backing.

FILET. Laced netting. Also known as lacis.

FLANNEL. Wool fabric, loosely woven.

FRIEZE. A woollen cloth with a nap used for wall hangings and upholstery.

FUSTIAN. Mixed cotton and linen fabric used for blankets.

GALLOON. A narrow ribbon of silk, silver or gold threads, used for trimming liveries and upholstery.

GINGHAM. Fabric (originally Indian) of cotton, linen or silk, distinguished by its checks and stripes. Used for dresses and on furniture.

GROSGRAM. Silk fabric, sometimes mixed with mohair or wool. Thick and strong and used in upholstery.

HARRATEEN. Worsted fabric used in eighteenth century for furnishing.

HOLLAND. Fine quality linen used for sheets and pillow cases.

KERSEY. Coarse twilled cloth used for chair coverings.

LACIS. See **FILET.**

LINEN. Fabric made from flax.

LINSEY WOOLSEY. Fabric woven from a mixture of wool and linen.

LUSTRING. A glossy light silk fabric used for upholstery.

MOCKADO. Imitation velvet used for curtains and upholstery.

MOHAIR. Fabric of silk or cotton mixed with wool from the angora goat. Used for all types of furnishings.

MOREEN. Woollen or woollen and cotton fabric used for curtains.

OSNABURG. A coarse linen, originally made in Osnabrück.

PARAGON. Coarse worsted fabric used on seats and for curtains.

PERPETUANA. Durable woollen fabric used for a lining and upholstery.

PHILIP AND CHINA or **CHEYNEY.** Brightly coloured worsted cloth used for wall hangings and chair coverings.

PILE. The nap on velvet or plush, formed by cutting the loops of the warp.

PINTADO. Painted or stained Indian cloth used for beds and wall coverings.

PLAID. Checked fabric from Scotland used for curtains and upholstery.

PLUSH. Silk, wool or cotton fabric with a long pile used for upholstery, table coverings, curtains and on livery uniforms.

REP. Strong fabric of cotton, wool or silk used for furniture upholstery and curtains.

RUSSET. A coarse woollen cloth of a reddish-brown, grey or neutral colour, used for blankets and the dress of peasantry.

SARSENET, SARCENET. Very fine and soft silk fabric used for fine work such as bed hangings and curtains.

SATIN, SATIN WEAVE. Silk fabric with a glossy surface on one side, only produced by the weaving method.

SAY. English fabric of twill weave used for bed and wall hangings.

SERGE. Wool and worsted fabric used in upholstery of beds and chairs.

SHAG. Worsted or silk fabric with a long pile used for the lining of mantles and coats, and also in upholstery.

SHALLOON. Cheap, closely-woven worsted fabric used for linings and upholstery.

SOUTHEGE. Coarse woven linen used for curtains and linings in the sixteenth and seventeenth centuries.

TICKING. Linen twill, often in herring-bone pattern, impervious to feathers and so used as covering for feather beds and pillows.

TISSUE. Expensive fabric often interwoven with gold or silver, used for royal bed hangings and in churches.

TWILL, TWILLED. A woven fabric which has parallel diagonal ridges.

VELVET. Silk fabric (sometimes cotton or wool) with short dense pile used for rich bed hangings and furniture upholstery.

VERMILION. Cotton or woollen cloth dyed scarlet used for hangings and beds.

WORSTED. Fine hard-wearing woollen fabric.

FURNITURE GLOSSARY

ACANTHUS. Mediterranean plant, *Acanthus spinosus*, with fleshy scalloped leaves. In stylized form found on Corinthian capitals and in the eighteenth century became a popular motif for furniture.

AIRWOOD. See HAREWOOD.

APRON. Extension below the bottom edge of the seat of a chair or the frame of a table or cabinet.

BACHELOR'S CHEST. Small chest with drawers or doors.

BAIL. Hooped handle or drawer pull hanging downward from pins attached to a metal plate.

BALUSTER. A short post supporting a rail and forming a balustrade.

BANDING. Ornamental or veneered border around doors, panels, drawers or table tops.

    CROSS-BANDING. The grain runs at right angles to the edge;

    FEATHER-BANDING and HERRINGBONE-BANDING are set at an angle;

    STRAIGHT-BANDING is cut along the length of the grain.

BEADING. Decorative border used on non-upholstered furniture, formed by a single row of round beads of the same size. If the round beads alternate with elongated beads, it is known as Bead-and-Reel.

BENTWOOD. Wood that is bent while wet into curved chair parts.

BERGÈRE Large, comfortable armchair with upholstered sides and loose cushion seat, popular in France in the Louis XV period. In eighteenth century England these chairs were known as burjairs or barjairs.

BOULLE or **BUHL MARQUETRY.** Brass and tortoiseshell marquetry, often set in an ebony ground, developed in France by André Charles Boulle. Fashionable throughout the eighteenth and nineteenth centuries.

BREAKFRONT CABINET. Cabinet divided vertically into three sections, with the middle section projecting forward.

BRONZE D'ORE. Gilded metal, especially cast brass or bronze gilded with an amalgam of gold and mercury, used to decorate furniture.

BUFFET. Sideboard or dresser for the dining room, designed to hold plates and serving dishes.

    BUFFET À GLISSANT ('sliding table'). A buffet which has a smaller, recessed compartment, known as the tabernacle, which has doors that slide out to the sides to open.

    BUFFET DE CHASSE ('hunting table'). A buffet table with a marble top, for preparing game.

    BUFFET DEUX CORPS ('two-bodied table'). A two-tiered buffet with the bottom cabinet deeper than the top one.

BUREAU. A desk with a lid sloping at an acute angle (usually about forty-five degrees) that folds out as a writing surface, with drawers underneath. If surmounted by a bookcase, it is known as a bureau-bookcase.

BURL. Veneer produced by slicing cross-sections of abnormal tree growths, usually walnut and elm.

BURR. Circular pattern in the grain of a piece of wood, caused by a growth on the trunk of the tree.

BUTLER'S TRAY. Tray of wood, silver or japanned metal mounted on a folding stand, popular in the eighteenth century.

CABRIOLE. Curved shape that resembles the leg of an animal, such as a goat (*cabriole* in Spanish). Its double curve turns in at the knee and out at the foot. Popular from the late seventeenth century.

CAMEL BACK. Chair back with a raised central curve.

CAMPAIGN FURNITURE. Portable furniture that folds flat or is made of components that can be disassembled. Originally for military use.

> CAMPAIGN CHAIR. Used by officers: a sling seat supported by a collapsible scissor structure.
>
> CAMPAIGN CHEST. Small chest with metal corners and flush hardware.

CANTERBURY. Stand with deep open partitions, sometimes with a drawer, for holding sheet music.

CAPSTAN TABLE. See DRUM TABLE.

CARCASE. Furniture used for storage. Also refers to the main structure of furniture to which veneers are applied.

CARD TABLE. Folding table that originated in the late seventeenth century.

CARLTON HOUSE TABLE or DESK. Writing table with small drawers above the surface forming a U-shape round the user instead of being merely set up in front of him. Designed by George Hepplewhite and named after writing tables at the Prince Regent's Carlton House.

CARTOUCHE. A scroll-shaped panel, sometimes bearing an inscription, monogram, or coat of arms, and used as a decorative feature.

CARVER. Dining chair with arms. From the nineteenth century.

CASE FURNITURE, CASE GOODS. Non-upholstered furniture, such as tables, dressers and bookcases.

CHAIR RAIL. Horizontal timber mould fixed to a wall to prevent damage to wall decoration when chairs are against it.

CHAISE LONGUE. Sofa or daybed with an upholstered back.

CHANNEL BACK. Chair back with grooves or fluting as decoration.

CHESTERFIELD. Couch with upholstered ends and no exposed wood. The back and arms usually form one continuous curve.

CHEST or **BLANKET CHEST.** Used for general storage, usually kept in the bedroom.

BLOCKFRONT CHEST. Chest-of-drawers in which the centre is concave and the end panels are convex.

BOWFRONT CHEST. Chest-of-drawers with a convex front.

CHEST-ON-CHEST. Chest-of-drawers in two sections, one on top of the other: a tallboy.

CHEVAL MIRROR. Mirror supported by posts which stand on the floor.

CHIFFONIER. Small cupboard with drawers inside the doors.

CLOSE STOOL. Movable lavatory with a hinged top which opens to reveal a pan. It was superseded by the night table. See also **COMMODE.**

CLUB SOFA. Upholstered sofa with a level back and lower arms.

COFFER. Travelling chest with handles and a domed lid but without feet, usually made of oak.

COLONETTE. A quarter- or half-round pilaster, fluted or reeded; frequently used in the late eighteenth century at the front corners of chests of drawers.

COMMODE. Initially a French chest of drawers, subsequently any type of low chest containing doors or drawers. From the mid nineteenth century the term was in use in England for a close stool.

CONSOLE TABLE. Table fixed to a wall, usually having a marble top, supported on shaped legs curving back to the wall.

CORNICE. Decorative, moulded projection at the top of a piece of furniture, particularly tall cupboards and display cabinets.

COURT CUPBOARD. Low (French *court*) shelved piece of furniture for displaying plate. Normally constructed in two stages, sometimes with a cupboard in the upper stage.

CREDENCE TABLE. Small table used for storing food before serving; generally a semicircular table with a hinged top.

CREDENZA. Long side cabinet with shelves on the ends, used for serving and storage.

CRESTING. Carved decoration surmounting a mirror or cabinet.

C–SCROLL. A decorative, carved or applied classical ornament in the shape of a C. An element of the Rococo style of the Georgian period.

DADO. Wood panelling running round the lower part of the walls of a room comprising a base, panelling, and a projecting chair rail.

DAVENPORT. Small writing-desk, often with a shallow sloped top and several drawers.

DAYBED. Sofa designed for resting rather than sleeping. It usually has one raised end.

DEMI-LUNE, HALF-MOON. Semicircular table commonly placed against the wall.

DENTIL PATTERN. Small rectangular blocks, resembling teeth, that run beneath a cornice.

DRESSER. Originally a table used to dress meats. Later, a cupboard for utensils and dishes.

DRESSING GLASS. Toilet mirror standing on a dressing-table.

DROP LEAF. Hinged flap that can be raised to increase the surface area of a table.

DROP LID DESK. Desk with a hinged panel that covers the inner compartments.

DRUM TABLE, CAPSTAN TABLE or RENT TABLE. Circular table with drawers, usually on a tripod base.

DUMB WAITER. Small serving table with a central shaft and circular trays, which often revolves to enable those who are dining to help themselves.

EBONIZED. Wood stained black to simulate ebony.

EGG-AND-DART. Classic carving motif of ornamental moulding in which an egg shape alternates with a dart.

ELBOW CHAIR. Armchair, particularly one with open arms and padded arm-rests.

ESCRITOIRE. Cabinet with a fall front that lowers to form a writing surface.

ESCUTCHEON. Ornamental plate surrounding a keyhole.

FALL FRONT. The front of a desk which forms a writing surface when lowered.

FESTOON. Ornament in the form of a garland of flowers or leaves.

FIELD BEDSTEAD or TENT BED. Small folding four-post bed.

FINIAL. End decoration used on upright posts, often of metal.

FLUTING. Parallel channels used on columns and legs. Often used on table legs in Neo-classical furniture.

FLY TABLE. Small table with extending flaps supported on gate-legs or hinged brackets.

FOOT, BALL-AND-CLAW or **CLAW-AND-BALL.** Carved foot motif depicting a crane's or eagle's claw gripping a ball or an egg. It is most associated with eighteenth century English and American furniture.

> BALL FOOT. Round foot used on oak and walnut case furniture and chairs during the late seventeenth and early eighteenth centuries.
>
> BLOCK FOOT. Cube-shaped foot used at the base of square-legged furniture.
>
> BUN FOOT. Flattened ball foot, used on furniture from the mid seventeenth century.
>
> BRACKET FOOT. Shaped foot on carcase furniture, which projects slightly at each corner. The bracket can be ornamented with beading.
>
> CLUB FOOT. Leg terminating in the form of a club (like a slightly pointed toe), usually thick and substantial.
>
> LION'S-PAW FOOT. Foot carved in the shape of a lion's paw, a popular Regency motif.
>
> SPADE FOOT. Rectangular, tapered foot separated from the rest of the leg by a slight projection.

GAINSBOROUGH CHAIR. Armchair with an upholstered seat and back, padded open arms and carved decoration.

GALLERY. Small decorative railing at the edge of a table or tray, usually of spindles between a top and bottom rail.

GATE-LEG TABLE. Table whose flaps are supported by jointed gates which swing out from the central section.

GESSO. A plaster-like composition of gypsum, size and glue, used to make a raised design on furniture. Usually gilded or painted.

GIRANDOLE. An ornate candlestick holder, often backed with a mirror.

GIRTH WEB. Woven hemp strips that support the stuffing of upholstered chairs.

GUERIDON. Small, round table used to support a candlestick or candelabrum.

GUILLOCHE. Carved decorative motif with a continuous band of strands twisted or braided together. First seen in classical architecture, the motif was popular with Neo-classical designers.

HALF-MOON. See **DEMI-LUNE.**

HAREWOOD or **AIRWOOD.** Veneer of sycamore wood dyed brownish-grey; used extensively in the late eighteenth century.

HARLEQUIN TABLE. Table in which a central nest of drawers in a square or oval frame is raised by weight or spring mechanisms, and pushed back flat with the table surface after use.

HARVEST TABLE. Narrow rectangular table with hinged drop-leaves.

HIGHBOY. Tall chest of drawers, usually in two sections: an upper chest on either a table-like structure or a lowboy with long legs.

> BONNET-TOP HIGHBOY. Highboy with a full dome or hood over the top of the piece.

HIPPED KNEE. Cabriole chair leg with carved ornament on the knee.

HUNTBOARD. Light, portable sideboard for serving food and drinks.

JAPANNING. Decorative technique, dating from the seventeenth century, in which furniture is coated with layers of coloured varnish in imitation of true Chinese or Japanese lacquer.

KNEEHOLE DESK, PEDESTAL DESK. Desk with a recessed central cupboard; or a desk with the top resting on a pair of pedestals with drawers.

KNOLE SETTEE. Settee with high back and hinged arms which are held upright when not in use by rope loops. Named after a seventeenth-century example at Knole Park, Kent and popular in the 1920s.

LADDER BACK or **SLAT BACK.** Chair with back posts joined by horizontal cross-rails.

LIBRARY CHAIR. Armchair with padded, leather covered, saddle-shaped seat. The back has an adjustable hinged flap to hold a book and compartments in the arms for pen and inks. The sitter usually straddles the seat facing the back.

LINENFOLD. Carved ornamentation on panelling or settee-backs imitating folded cloth. Popular in the sixteenth and seventeenth centuries.

LIVERY CUPBOARD. Sixteenth and seventeenth century cupboard which housed night snacks (bread, beer, spiced wine), drinking vessels and candles.

LOO TABLE. Large oval or circular card table with a central support and tip-up top.

LOVESEAT. Double chair or small sofa.

LOWBOY. Small dressing table.

MARQUETRY. Inlay of unusual woods, mother-of-pearl, etc into a veneered surface.

MARQUISE. A broad chair to accommodate the wide skirts of women in the eighteenth century.

MOTHER-OF-PEARL. Lining of certain shells used as an inlay for furniture, particularly in the nineteenth century.

MULE CHEST. Chest with drawers in the base; forerunner of the chest-of-drawers.

MUNTIN. Vertical wooden member between two panels.

NECESSARY STOOL. A close stool with a hinged top.

NIGHT TABLE. A bedside pot cupboard, often with a tray top, and a necessary stool that pulls forward in the lower part.

NONSUCH CHEST. Sixteenth century chest richly decorated with marquetry patterns of arches and fantastic architecture. Named after Henry VIII's palace of Nonsuch.

ORMOLU. Gilt bronze, used for furniture mounts and door furniture.

OTTOMAN. Early eighteenth century upholstered bench.

PARCEL-GILT. Selective gilding of decorative elements.

PARQUETRY. Furniture veneering in a decorative, geometric pattern.

PATERA. Neo-classical motif, oval or round, resembling a flower or rosette.

PATTERN CHAIR. Model from which to work, frequently with arms or legs showing alternate forms of decoration.

PEDESTAL DESK. See **KNEEHOLE DESK.**

PEDESTAL TABLE. Table supported by a single central column.

PEDIMENT. Originally the triangular gable above the portico of a classical temple. Adapted in various forms for the tops of furniture.

> BROKEN PEDIMENT. Has a central break in base or apex, to incorporate a bust.

PEMBROKE TABLE. Eighteenth century small rectangular drop-leaf table with a drawer, named after the Earl of Pembroke.

PENCIL-POST BED. Bed with four slim posts, either standing alone or with a canopy.

PIE-CRUST. Raised edge to tables resembling a pie-crust.

PIER TABLE. Table designed to stand against a wall, hence often semicircular in shape; often surmounted by a PIER MIRROR.

PILASTER. A column attached to the wall, i.e. semicircular in section.

POLE SCREEN. Fire screen mounted on a pole, with a tripod or platform base. The screen may be moved vertically and locked at various heights.

PRESS BEDSTEAD. A folding bedstead built into a cabinet looking like a press or chest.

PUTTO. A cherub. A motif widely used during the Renaissance and in particular during the seventeenth century.

RAIL. Any horizontal timber member.

RÉCAMIER. Early nineteenth century daybed with a curved headboard and shorter curved footboard. Named after Mme Récamier (1777–1840), leading Parisian socialite of the early nineteenth century.

REEDING Consecutive parallel convex curves formed for vertical or horizontal decoration on chair and table legs, borders and edgings. The opposite of FLUTING.

RENT TABLE. See DRUM TABLE.

ROCAILLE. Rock and shell forms characteristic of the Rococo style.

SCAGLIOLA. Plaster-like substance, to which are added colour pigments and small pieces of stone such as granite, marble, and alabaster so that it can be polished to look like marble.

SECRETARY or SECRÉTAIRE. Writing cabinet. It often has a slim drawer beneath the top, and a fall-front writing surface. Popular during the eighteenth century.

SERPENTINE. Furniture characterized by an undulating front, with a convex central surface and concave ends.

SETTEE. Dates from the seventeenth century and preceded the sofa.

SHIELD-BACK CHAIR. Chair where the rail and stile form the shape of a shield. Made popular by George Hepplewhite in the 1780s.

SIDE CHAIR. Small chair without arms, designed to stand against a wall.

SIDE TABLE. Table designed to stand against a wall, frequently acting as a secondary serving table.

SLAT-BACK CHAIR. See LADDER-BACK.

SLEIGH BED. Bed in which the head and footboards are scrolled. It originated in America in the early nineteenth century.

SLIPPER CHAIR. High-backed, usually upholstered chair with short legs, developed in America in the eighteenth century for bedrooms.

SOFA. Long seat with back and arms. Less formal and longer than a settee, it became very popular by the early 1800s.

SOFA TABLE. Long, narrow table with drawers and drop-leaf ends, typically used to play and store board games.

SPINDLE. Slim length of turned wood, often used in a series for chair backs.

SPLAT. Vertical member between the seat and top rail of a chair.

SQUAB. Removable stuffed cushion for a chair or stool.

S−SCROLL. Carved or applied classical ornament in the shape of an S. An element of the Rococo style of the Georgian period

STATE BED. A grand, lavishly upholstered bed intended for princes and noblemen.

STRAP-WORK. Stylized representation of geometrically arranged leather straps.

STRETCHER. Horizontal timber member bracing the legs of furniture.

STRINGING. Narrow band of wood inlay. In the Regency period brass was sometimes used.

SUSSEX CHAIR. Chair with an ash frame and rush seat, based on a traditional country design.

SUTHERLAND TABLE. Small swing-leg drop-leaf table. The central portion is very narrow.

SWAN NECK. Ogee (S−shaped) curve.

TAMBOUR DESK. Rolltop desk with a flexible, draw-down cover made of tambours, a succession of narrow strips of flat wood glued to stiff cloth.

TEA POY. Small stand on a column frequently set on a foot of four splayed legs, with a hinged compartment for tea-caddies.

TENT BEDSTEAD. See **FIELD BEDSTEAD**.

TESTER. Canopy over a bedstead supported on the bedposts.

> ANGEL CANOPY. A canopy suspended from the ceiling on chains.
>
> HALF-TESTER. A short canopy projecting from the headboard and otherwise unsupported.

TORCHERE. Torch-holder, tall candelabrum or hall lamp; sometimes, a stand supporting a lamp.

TRIPOD TABLE. Small table with a round top supported by a pillar which branches into three feet.

TUNBRIDGE WARE. Form of marquetry decoration. Pieces of different coloured woods were glued together so that the ends formed a pattern and the block was then sliced transversely, making up to thirty identical slices. Originated in Tunbridge Wells in the seventeenth century.

TURKEY WORK. Imitation oriental carpet. The wool was drawn through a canvas and knotted to form a pile. Usually found on chair seats as upholstery.

VALANCE. Short curtain around the canopy of a bed.

VENEER. Thin layer of fine wood that is applied to the surface of a more durable wood, for decorative effect. Veneers were widely used from the second half of the seventeenth century onward.

VITRINE. China or curio cabinet with glass doors.

WAINSCOT. Wood panelling generally, but especially panelling which goes up to chair-rail height only.

WAINSCOT CHAIR. Early chair with a panelled back, open arms and wood seat.

WELLINGTON CHEST. Tall, narrow, plain chest named after the first Duke of Wellington.

WHATNOT. A stand with small shelves, sometimes incorporating a drawer.

WINDSOR CHAIR. Chair with a spindle back and legs, usually with arms.

WING BACK CHAIR or **WING CHAIR.** Fully upholstered chair with wings at the sides to protect the sitter from drafts.

BEDS

The main bedroom in large houses also served as a reception room until the end of the eighteenth century. Consequently, the quality of the bed and its furnishings were important status symbols. Such beds were often raised on a dais, sometimes in an alcove separated from the rest of the room by a balustrade. The early beds had a wooden frame, often with posts, a covering over the top fixed to the posts or hung from the ceiling, and a board behind the pillows. Two sets of valances around the bed concealed the curtain rings and pulleys. The most luxurious bed fillings were goose feathers and swan's down. Queen Anne's bedding, which included 90 lbs of swan's down, cost £18 10s in 1705 (£30,000 today). The feather beds were placed over one or more mattresses filled with coarser material such as hair or straw.

In the mid-eighteenth century French beds became popular. Instead of posts, a bracket was fixed to the wall from which draperies could be hung and the bed was then often placed parallel to the wall. Finer materials such as cotton and linen were now used for the bed hangings. Metal beds also became available and increased in popularity—they proved less inviting to bed bugs than their predecessors.

The requirements for a good night's sleep in a four-poster have not changed that much over time. Apart from the bed itself, sheets, blankets, a cover and a pillow comprise the essentials. The best sheets have always been made of linen. In the sixteenth and seventeenth centuries, those from the Low Countries (cambric) and Northern France were particularly prized. But only luminaries such as heads of households or guests might sleep between these sheets. Lesser members of the family and servants had to make do with coarser materials.

The fabrics and fashions of blankets and bed coverings have been more susceptible to change. Early blankets were made of fustian and nearly every bed had a pair. In the sixteenth century blanket cloth (all wool) was used. The most expensive were those made from the wool of Merino sheep. Later, blankets were made from many different materials such as fustian cotton, linsey woolsey, and russet, but by the end of the eighteenth century wool was again the preferred material. Bed coverings were made from darnix until the introduction of Indian cotton in the seventeenth century. Machine-woven counterpanes arrived with industrialisation, and by the mid-nineteenth century ones made from machine-embroidered silk were favoured for the better beds.

BEDS WORTH SLEEPING IN

White Room bed at Cotehele House, Cornwall (fifteenth to early sixteenth centuries).

King's bed and Venetian Ambassador's bed at Knole Park, Kent (sixteenth century).

State bed at Hardwick Hall, Derbys (1597).

State bed in the Damask Bedchamber, and Blathwayt's bed in the Tapestry Bedchamber at Dyrham Park, Glos (1692–1704).

Daniel Marot bed at Clandon Park, Surrey (1730–3).

Slate bed at Penrhyn Castle, Gwynedd, weighing more than one ton and built for a visit by Queen Victoria (1859).

CLOCKS

Mechanical clocks first appeared in the second half of the thirteenth century in Eastern Europe. They were large, iron, blacksmith-made machines. Their main function was to strike a bell (for monasteries and churches) and they did not have any hands or dial face. The Salisbury Cathedral clock, built in 1386, is considered to be the world's oldest surviving mechanical clock that strikes the hours. Domestic clocks appeared soon afterwards: the earliest domestic clock in England is at Cotehele House, Cornwall and was installed by Sir Richard Edgecumbe in the 1480s.

Until around 1450 all clocks were weight-driven and had to be fixed in position. It was at this time that a coiled spring was first used in clock mechanisms. By 1500 clocks were still extremely inaccurate, but their more elaborate designs made them highly-prized objects. Accuracy only improved with the introduction of the pendulum clock in the seventeenth century. The first pendulum was fitted to a clock in 1657 by the Dutch scientist Christiaan Huygens and pendulum clocks were introduced to England by John Fromanteel in 1660. A subsequent improvement to the accuracy of the pendulum clock, using an anchor escapement which works by reducing the arc of the pendulum swing, resulted in the appearance of the English longcase (or grandfather) clock in 1680.

The beginnings of mass production appeared in the eighteenth century. Movement 'blanks' were made for sale to clock or watch 'finishers', who then sold on complete clock movements; specialist craftsmen made the cases and others the painted dials. The nineteenth century saw the full mass production of cheap clocks, first in the Black Forest area of Germany, and then in the USA, which became the main source of inexpensive shelf clocks.

The best collections of clocks are in: the British Museum, the Science Museum, and the Clockmakers' Company, all in London; the Ashmolean Museum, Oxford; and the Fitzwilliam Museum, Cambridge. Among country houses, Belmont House, Kent (1769–93) is reputed to have the best collection of clocks in the UK. Other good collections are at: Lyme Park and Dunham Massey Hall, both in Cheshire; Trerice, Cornwall; Anglesey Abbey, Cambs; Attingham Park, Salop; Shugborough Hall, Staffs; and Snowshill Manor, Glos.

TYPES OF CLOCKS

BALLOON CLOCK. A clock with case shaped like a hot-air balloon of the late eighteenth century.

CARRIAGE CLOCK. An eighteenth century carriage clock originally designed to be carried easily for use when travelling. It typically has a brass frame with four glass sides and top and a carrying handle. France was especially known for the production of these clocks in the mid to late nineteenth century.

CUCKOO CLOCK. A German invention of the 1730s, these became popular in the third quarter of the nineteenth century.

DROP DIAL, DROP TRUNK, or **'SCHOOLHOUSE'** clock. A clock with a trunk extension that houses a pendulum. The trunk usually has a door with a glass window, allowing the pendulum's movement to be easily adjusted and seen.

GRANDMOTHER CLOCK. A shorter version of the grandfather clock.

LANTERN CLOCK. An English weight-driven clock style dating from the early 1600s. One of the first clocks with a movement and external structure made predominantly from brass instead of iron or wood.

SHELF CLOCK. A clock with a case designed to sit on a shelf, table or mantelpiece, as opposite to a longcase clock or a wall clock.

SKELETON CLOCK. The movement of a skeleton clock is visible as a decorative object in itself. Late eighteenth and early nineteenth century.

TAVERN CLOCK. A large-dialled clock, with a trunk below to house the pendulum and weights. Common from about 1725 to 1800 in public places and in the servants' halls of large private houses.

VIENNA REGULATOR or **VIENNA TYPE WALL CLOCK.** A very accurate, weight-driven wall clock produced in Austria during the early nineteenth century.

SILVER

As silver is a precious metal, silver objects are more exposed to hazards of time and chance than those made of the baser metals. The family silver was often sold to be melted down and re-used, or confiscated by an avaricious government, or, in the twentieth century, given to the state in settlement of death duties.

From the Middle Ages to the sixteeenth century buffets of plate—displays of vessels in precious metals—were common in the dining halls of the nobility. But such early pieces are rarely found now outside major museums, Oxford and Cambridge colleges, livery companies and the Church.

The grandest plate of the early seventeenth century was silver furniture. Nell Gwyn's silver bed contained over two thousand ounces of silver and cost £1,135 (about £1,702,000 today). A silver furniture suite can be seen at Knole Park, Kent, and there are good collections of silver at Attingham Park, Salop (ambassadorial plate of the Regency period), Dunham Massey Hall, Ches, and Ickworth House, Suffolk (early to mid eighteenth century).

Individual pieces may be found in all of the largest houses including Blenheim Palace, Oxon (silver centrepiece of the Duke of Marlborough on horseback), Burghley House, Lincs (early eighteenth century wine cooler made with 230 lbs of silver), and Chatsworth House, Derbys (early eighteenth century banqueting pieces).

SILVER HALLMARKS

1300 First mark struck on silver, a leopard's head, as a London assay mark.

1363 Second mark, a maker's mark, introduced.

1457 Edinburgh Assay office established (three-towered castle mark; changed to a thistle in 1759).

London   Edinburgh   Newcastle   Exeter   Sheffield   Birmingham

1478 A third mark indicating the year added (a letter of the alphabet, changed annually on 19 May, the feast of St Dunstan, patron saint of goldsmiths).

1544 A fourth mark, a lion passant, was added, indicating the item was of standard silver.

1700 Newcastle Assay Office established (three castles mark), closed 1884.

1701 York office established (St. George's cross charged with five lion passants mark), closed 1716. Exeter Assay office established (three-turreted castle mark), closed 1883.

1773 Sheffield Assay office established (with crown as mark); Birmingham office established (anchor mark).

1819 Glasgow Assay office established (a tree, a fish and a bell), closed 1964.

COMMON TYPES OF SILVER VESSELS AND OBJECTS

ANDIRONS. A pair of log stands with decorative vertical element at the front, in iron, brass or silver. Popular in England until the eighteenth century, when coal generally replaced wood fires.

ARGYLL. A small jug with an inner chamber filled with hot water, for keeping gravy hot while on the table. First recorded around 1760; possibly originally made for the use of the fourth Duke of Argyll.

BUFFET OF PLATE. A display of precious vessels in the halls of princes, nobility and great ecclesiastics during the Middle Ages and the sixteenth century.

CASTER. A container with a pierced cover for sprinkling sugar, salt or ground pepper.

CAUDLE CUP, POSSET CUP. A two-handled vessel for drinking warm spiced gruel.

CHAMBER CANDLESTICK. A portable candlestick on a plate-shaped base with a scroll or ring handle.

CHARGER. A large, shallow plate for serving meat.

COASTER. A small tray for circulating food or bottles at the dining table. Also describes a circular decanter stand with silver sides.

CRUET. A small bottle, usually with a stopper, used for oil and vinegar in houses and for wine and water in church.

CRUET FRAME. A silver stand holding several bottles or two bottles and three casters.

    WARWICK CRUET FRAME. Usually for three casters and four bottles.

EWER. A large jug with a wide mouth.

    HELMET EWER. Shaped like an inverted Roman helmet, with ovoid body on a low stem; particularly favoured by Huguenot goldsmiths.

FLATWARE. Usually spoons, forks and cutlery but sometimes extended to other non-hollow ware, such as salvers.

KNOP. A decorative bulbous moulding in the stem of a cup.

MAZARINE. A flat plate, pierced to drain fish. Often elaborately engraved.

MONTEITH. A cooler for wine glasses. The glasses were held in the notched rim of the bowl, with the feet in water.

MUFFINEER. A small, plain caster, made of silver or brass and often with a scroll handle. Late seventeenth and early eighteenth centuries.

PLATE. Wrought silver or gold.

PORRINGER. A small shallow bowl with one or two flat handles. Also refers to a deeper bowl, often covered, with two scroll handles and made mainly of silver.

POSSET CUP. See **CAUDLE CUP.**

SALVER. A tray, sometimes with feet, for serving food or drink.

SCONCE. A bracket candlestick with mirror or polished back-plate to reflect light.

SHEFFIELD PLATE. A copper plate coated with silver.

SKILLET. A saucepan with three feet and a long handle. Silver skillets survive from the mid seventeenth century.

SNUFFERS. Scissors with a box at the end, for trimming candle wicks.

STANDISH. An inkstand, fitted with an inkwell, a sand box and, until the mid eighteenth century, a bell.

TANKARD. A beer mug with a hinged lid.

PORTRAIT PAINTING

Portraits were hung traditionally in three locations in country houses: in halls (including entrance halls), dining rooms, and long galleries. In the latter, they competed with other objects such as statuary and tapestries. Even where houses were built or enlarged to take collections, such as Burghley House, Lincs, Houghton Hall, Beds, and Kedleston Hall, Derbys, dedicated picture galleries were not at first included. Instead, as collections grew, pictures were distributed throughout the house. It was only in the early nineteenth century that purpose-built picture galleries became popular. Colt Hoare added a picture gallery to Stourhead House, Wilts, at this time.

To have your portrait painted became *de rigeur* for the English aristocracy from the sixteenth century onwards. Such portraits were symbols of power, status, and lineage. Court painters such as Hans Holbein the Younger (a favourite of Henry VIII) were also popular with the wealthier classes, both nobility and merchants, while there were plenty of imitators for the middle classes. By the end of the century full-length portraits on canvas were hanging in the long galleries of country houses such as Hardwick Hall, Derbys, Kenwood House, London, and Penshurst Place, Kent.

The Georgian period was the heyday of portrait hanging in country houses. The major Georgian portrait painters such as Sir

Joshua Reynolds worked primarily in London, where they catered to a flourishing demand among the aristocracy and middle classes. Provincial towns also has their portrait painters including Thomas Gainsborough in Bath and Philippe Mercier in York.

Portrait painting continued to be popular in the Victorian period, although by the end of the nineteenth century it was competing with photography. Most recently it has embraced the digital age: Chatsworth House, Derbys, unveiled its latest portrait in 2010—a 'Computer Portrait of Laura Burlington'—one where the colours constantly change.

Full length portraits may be viewed in the Ballroom, Knole Park, Kent, and Hardwick Hall, Derbys where they compete with tapestries. There are picture galleries at Ham House, Surrey, Chirk Castle, Den, and Althorp House, Northants. Waddesdon Manor, Bucks, holds full-length eighteenth-century portraits in the nineteenth-century Rothschild collection. Portraits of servants - Erdigg Hall, Cheshire

---

COATS OF ARMS

Heraldic symbols such as coats of arms are outward signs of aristocratic and hereditary status. Henry III copied the idea from France in the thirteenth century, creating coats of arms for the royal family and the nobles at court.

A full coat of arms comprises: a shield with its symbols (devices or charges), supported by figures on either side, with a helmet and crest above, and mottoes below. Badges of rank may also appear.

Coats of arms are often displayed over the entrances to country houses, or in the hall. They were incorporated into architectural features, for example as part of the decoration on a ceiling, or displayed in many other contexts, such as on the livery of servants, coaches, furniture, silver, porcelain, and bookplates.

Coats of arms were much displayed in the sixteenth and seventeenth centuries, but became subject to the vagaries of fashion. During the Greek Revival, their use as exterior ornamentation declined, while the Gothic Revival led to increased interest and to the extensive use of heraldic symbols in Victorian country houses.

GARDEN GLOSSARY

The mediaeval garden was principally utilitarian (although tastefully arranged), growing herbs, fruit and vegetables, interspersed with paths and lawns. The pleasure garden was an Italian Renaissance rediscovery based on the accounts of the ancients: the gardens of the Medici Villa at Fiesole (1455–61) and the Palazzo Piccolomini at Pienza (1459) are examples which were swiftly followed elsewhere. The gardens of Le Nôtre (1613–1700) in France were a extension of the Italian model, featuring flat ground, a central house, a central axis, and plenty of statues and water features. Gardens in the United Kingdom were in this formal style until the advent of William Kent (c.1685–1748) and 'Capability' Brown (1716 83). They introduced the 'naturalised' garden, with artificial lakes and 'randomly' planted groups of trees. Their work was continued by Humphrey Repton (1752–1818) and William Gilpin (1762–1843). New discoveries from around the world made their appearance from the 1820s ('gardenesque'). Gertrude Jekyll planted her first gardens in the 1890s: she introduced the herbaceous border and an impression of wild, colourful 'cottagey' gardens. Her influence continues.

✳ & compartmented gardens

ALLÉE. An outdoor long gallery for promenading: a long walk, often of lime or yew, sometimes with metal or timber supports.
  Melbourne Hall, Derbys (yew allée at planted 1704, reckoned to be the longest in Europe); Chatsworth House, Derbys; Hidcote Manor, Glos; and Bodnant Garden, Conwy.
AVENUE. Originally (late seventeenth century), the main approach to the house. It was normally a straight drive, the longer the better (e.g. Badminton House, Glos and Wimpole Hall, Cambs); but often, as at Castle Howard, N. Yorks, took advantage of undulations in the landscape to create spectacular surprises.
CARPET-BEDDING. See KNOT GARDEN.
CONSERVATION WALL. See HOT WALL.
CRINKLE-CRANKLE or CRINKUM-CRANKUM wall. Serpentine wall facing north–south against which fruit was grown. The serpentine

shape provided a larger south-facing surface than would be available with a straight wall.

FERNERY. A building specially constructed for ferns, normally on a distant part of the estate. This was a building peculiar to the Victorians and did not outlast the nineteenth century. There are few surviving examples.

Brodsworth Hall, W. Yorks; Tatton Park, Ches; Peckover House, Cambs; and Ashridge House, Herts.

HA-HA. A ditch separating the garden from the surrounding farmland. It was constructed with a wall on the garden side and a gentle slope rising to ground level on the farmland side.

HOTHOUSE, GLASSHOUSE. Greenhouse.

HOT WALL, CONSERVATION WALL. South-facing brick wall in a kitchen garden, containing horizontal flues heated from a stove. This encourages fruit to ripen earlier and protects them against frost.

KITCHEN GARDEN. Garden for fruit, vegetables and herbs. Introduced from France in the seventeenth century, it became a walled garden and a place for perambulation. After the First World War, the decline of large households meant the decline of kitchen gardens and very few remain today.

Stourhead House, Wilts (created early nineteenth century) and Calke Abbey, Derbys.

KNOT GARDEN. A bed in which dwarf plants of different colours are arranged to form a hedge with the spaces between filled with coloured earth or sand, or plants of different colours: like needlework (knot garden) or a carpet (carpet-bedding).

MAZE. A labyrinth. Its origins are very ancient, but with the rise of topiary it increased in popularity.

Hampton Court Palace, London (1699); Hever Castle, Kent; and Hatfield House, Herts.

MOUND. An artificial hill, often crowned with a gazebo, providing a view of the landscape beyond the garden.

PARTERRE. A level space in a garden filled with formal flower beds. Some were immense. Many were destroyed by the fashion for 'Capability' Brown's Picturesque (about 1750 onwards), although they made a gradual comeback from about 1820.

Blickling Hall, Norfolk (laid out 1872); Cliveden House, Bucks (one of the largest in Europe); The Great Garden at Pitmedden House, Aberdeenshire
Witley Court (Worcs)

(planted 1675, recreated 1950s); and Drummond Castle, Perth and Kinross (recreated 1820s and 1830s). Trentham Park also restored Italian style from 2004 a vast parterre

PERGOLA. Formed of plants trained over trellis-work, frequently forming a covered pathway.

ROCK GARDEN. An Alpine garden set among an artificial arrangement of rocks. Came into fashion with the Romantic Movement of the late eighteenth century and was further inspired by Robinson's *Alpine flowers for English gardens* (1870).

Killerton House, Devon (c.1910) and Leonardslee House, Sussex (late nineteenth century).

TOPIARY. The art of clipping trees and shrubs into ornamental shapes, such as animals, globes, and spirals. Popular in Britain since the sixteenth century, it was especially in vogue after the Glorious Revolution (1688) as the Dutch were experts in the craft.

Hampton Court Palace, London; Melbourne Hall, Derbys; Levens Hall, Cumb; Elvaston Hall, Derbys; Hidcote Manor, Glos; and Nymans, Sussex.

WILDERNESS. In the sixteenth and seventeenth centuries, an area of woodland, with the trees clipped and formally arranged. In later use, the area was far more 'natural' and often used as a contrast to parterres.

Ashridge House, Herts; Bodnant Garden, Conwy; and The Nuttery, Sissinghurst Castle, Kent. Hanbury Hall, Worcs.

ESTATE BUILDINGS

The estate buildings listed here have two origins. Buildings such as the estate yard, the stew pond and the dovecote were derived from, or imitate, mediaeval working structures. Others, such as the eye-catcher, the gazebo and the rotunda, were introduced from the beginning of the eighteenth century as part of the 'naturalisation' of the landscape, and sought to compose it with artfully placed buildings.

The name of the architect, where known, is given in brackets.

BELVEDERE. A room built on the roof of a country house to take advantage of the views. See also **GAZEBO.**

Belvedere tower, Melbury House, Dorset (c.1535); The Belvedere, Claremont House, Surrey (1716, Vanbrugh); and The Lantern, Lyme Park, Ches (c.1700).

BOTHY. See **GARDENER'S BOTHY.**

CONSERVATORY. A glass building, often with underfloor heating, in which plants needing protection from the cold were kept. It was frequently attached to the house, a more solid building than the hothouse, and designed for recreation and enjoyment, not merely for protecting plants.

Duncombe Park, N. Yorks (1851); Tatton Park, Ches (1818); and Witley Court, Worcs (1850s).

DOVECOTE. A (usually) round building in which pigeons were reared and kept for food during winter. It had nesting boxes around the wall, the highest of which were reached by a rotating ladder (a potence).

Kinwarton, Warwicks (fourteenth century, possibly the oldest in England); Snowshill Manor, Glos (c.1600, but dovecote is Late Mediaeval and still in use); Cotehele House, Cornwall (?fifteenth century); Hawford, Worcs (sixteenth century); Willington, Beds (sixteenth century); and Felbrigg, Norfolk (1753).

ESTATE OFFICE. The headquarters of the estate manager or steward, sometimes located within the main house, as at Lanhydrock, Cornwall, but more frequently in the estate yard, as at Lyme Park, Ches.

ESTATE YARD. The working heart of the estate: might have contained a smithy, wagon sheds, sawmill, joiner's shop and estate office.

Erddig, Den (c.1820, where the estate yard is almost intact); Calke Abbey, Beds (1704); and Stourhead House, Wilts (mid-eighteenth century).

EYE-CATCHER. A structure that intentionally draws the eye.

Worcester Lodge, Badminton House, Glos (c.1740, William Kent); The Dog Kennel, Chatelherault, Lanarkshire (c.1732, William Adam); and The Pineapple, Dunmore Park, Stirling (1761).

FABRIQUE. A building or other structure in a landscaped garden, such as an eye-catcher, folly, temple, ruin.

FISHING HOUSE, FISHING PAVILION. Usually, a single reception room on the edge of a lake, with windows from which ladies could fish. Heard of towards the end of the sixteenth century but really came into fashion in the mid-eighteenth.

Kedleston Hall, Derbys (1769); The Quarters, Alresford, Essex (1765, Richard Woods); Fort Henry, Exton Park, Rut (c.1795); and The Pavilion, Syon House, London (1802–8).

FOLLY. An otherwise useless building, such as a sham ruin, classical temple, tower, or Chinese pagoda, placed for purely compositional purposes in a Picturesque landscape garden.

GARDENER'S BOTHY. Head gardener's headquarters. In some cases, a communal living area for the garden lads.

Calke Abbey, Derbys (eighteenth century) and Lyme Park, Ches (c.1900).

GATEHOUSE, LODGE. Originally (late sixteenth century) a porter's lodge guarding a forecourt, later the gatehouse or lodge(s) moved to the entrance to the park and was more ceremonial than practical.

Charlecote Park, Warwicks (c.1550); Worcester Lodge, Badminton House, Glos (c.1740); Wentworth Woodhouse, S. Yorks (eighteenth century); Attingham Park, Salop (1785); The Gothick Lodge, Milton Hall, Cambs (1790s); and Fonthill Abbey, Wilts (c.1800).

GAZEBO. A small viewing tower, or a summer-house with a view. See also **BELVEDERE.**

Alkerton Grange, Glos (early eighteenth century) and Westbury Court Garden, Glos (mid eighteenth century).

GROTTO. An artificial or natural cave, usually near a lake, often near the head of it.

Nymph of the Grotto, Stourhead House, Wilts (1748); Claremont House, Surrey (1730s); Painshill Park, Surrey (c.1750); and Hampton Court House, Surrey (1767).

HUNTING BOX, HUNTING LODGE. A (usually) small house with stabling for occupation during the hunting season.

Worksop Manor Lodge, Notts (1590s: currently under restoration); Ashdown House, Berks (1660s); The Cage, Lyme Park, Ches (1737); and The Chateau, Gate Burton, Lincs (1747).

ICEHOUSE. A brick- or stone-lined pit, about twenty-five feet deep, with a drain at the bottom, covered by a dome-shaped superstructure with an entrance on the north side, in which blocks of ice could be kept for up to three years between layers of straw. Often situated beside a lake, from which the blocks of ice were cut in winter. It was introduced to England about 1660 and became redundant when hand-cranked ice-making machines appeared (1840s).

Ayscoughfee Hall, Lincs (early eighteenth century); Stourhead House, Wilts (mid eighteenth century); Heveningham Hall, Suffolk (eighteenth century); Killerton House, Devon (?nineteenth century); Rufford Abbey, Notts (c.1820); Danny House, Sussex (nineteenth century).

KIOSK. Summer-house or open pavilion, reminiscent of eastern models.

The Chinese House, Amesbury Abbey, Wilts (1765) and The Chinese Tent, Boughton House, Northants (mid-eighteenth century).

LODGE. See **GATEHOUSE.**

MAUSOLEUM. A monument built to receive a body or bodies.

Castle Howard, N. Yorks, (1728, perhaps the earliest. Designed by Nicholas Hawksmoor, but unfinished at his death in 1736); Brocklesby Park, Lincs (1787–92, James Wyatt); Bowood House, Wilts (1761, Robert Adam); and Blickling Hall, Norfolk (after 1793, Joseph Bonomi). Trentham Park / Hall

ORANGERY. Mostly eighteenth century. South-facing building, often attached to the house, for growing orange trees and other citrus fruits. Later, the orangery gave way to the conservatory.

Peckover House, Cambs (1722); The Gothick Orangery, Frampton Court, Glos (c.1750); The Orangery, Margam Castle, Glam (c.1790); and The Orangery (Decimus Burton), Glevering Hall, Suffolk (1830s).

PROSPECT TOWER. See **GAZEBO.**

ROTUNDA. A folly round in shape, normally with a dome.

Ionic and Doric Temples at Duncombe Park, N. Yorks (early eighteenth century); Temple of Venus, Hall Barn, Bucks (1720s, Colen Campbell); and Croome Court, Worcs (c.1750).

STABLES. Accommodation for horses from about the beginning of the seventeenth century, and for coaches from the beginning of the eighteenth century. Stables were usually built round a courtyard, with an entrance crowned with a cupola, often with a clock. Stable were often luxurious: those at Avery Hill, London (1880s) were centrally heated.

Calke Abbey, Derbys (c.1710); Blenheim Palace, Oxon (c.1720); Seaton Delaval Hall, Northumb (1718); Kedleston Hall, Derbys (1760s); and Wimpole Hall, Cambs (1851).

STEW, STEW POND. Fish pond, originally a monastic structure, built to keep carp and other fish as food.

Cotehele, Cornwall (Mediaeval).

SUMMER-HOUSE. A simple building, often rustic in appearance, providing shade, or a view, or a feature in a Picturesque landscape.

Burghley House, Lincs (1756, 'Capability' Brown); Gothic Temple, Bramham Park, W. Yorks (1750).

TACK ROOM. Room forming part of the stables, in which saddlery and other riding equipment were kept and cleaned.

Cronkhill, Salop, (1805, John Nash), Charlecote Park, Warwicks (nineteenth century).

TEMPLE. A folly in the shape of a Greek, Roman or Gothic temple, common in the seventeenth and eighteenth centuries.

Gothic Temple at Stowe House, Bucks, (1742); Doric Temple at Shugborough Hall, Staffs (1760s); Pantheon at Stourhead House, Wilts (mid eighteenth century); Gothic Temple (1750) and Paine's Temple, Bramham Park, W. Yorks (c.1760, James Paine); Temple of Victory, Audley End, Cambs (1771–2, Robert Adam); The Temple, Aske Hall, N. Yorks (1727–53); Temple of the Four Winds, Castle Howard (1724–6, Vanbrugh); Temple of Romulus and Remus, Coleby Hall, Lincs (c.1762, Sir William Chambers); and Mussenden Temple, Downhill, Co. Derry (1785).

TOWER. Normally built as a folly for the views from the top.

Vandalian Tower, Uppark (1774; ruined); Oval Pavilion, Farnborough Hall, Warwicks (c.1750); Horton Tower, Dorset (c.1765); King Alfred's Tower, Stourhead House, Wilts (1765–72); and Broadway Tower, Worcs (1799).

TRIUMPHAL ARCH. Part entrance gateway, part folly, part eye-catcher.

Holkham Hall, Norfolk (c.1735, William Kent) and Fonthill Abbey, Wilts (1757–70).

DUKES AND THEIR STATELY HOMES

The upper and historically the oldest ranks of the English nobility are collectively known as the Peerage of England. This includes all those whose titles were bestowed by the Kings and Queens of England before the Act of Union in 1707. Similarly the Peerage of

As at 2015 There are 24 non-royal Dukes. It is most likely that no more will be created so the title will gradually fade away. The first Dukedom was created by Queen Victoria in 1889 ... Dukedoms are granted by the monarch and once a Duke you can't resign the title, but of course the title is inherited in the male line ..

Scotland is all pre-1707 titles. Those added to the peerage between the 1707 Act of Union (England/Scotland) and the 1800 Act of Union (England/Ireland) comprise the Peerage of Great Britain. Those after 1800 belong to the Peerage of the United Kingdom, by which title the Peerage is collectively known today.

The five grades of the Peerage are: duke, marquess, earl, viscount, and baron. There are 24 dukes in the Peerage of the United Kingdom (excluding the royal dukes), 34 marquesses, 191 earls and 4 countesses in their own right, 115 viscounts, and 426 hereditary barons.

Several peerages may be held at the same time by one person and five dukes have more than one dukedom. They are: the Duke of Cornwall and Rothesay (i.e. the Prince of Wales); the Duke of Hamilton (in the Peerage of Scotland) and Brandon (in the peerage of Great Britain); the Duke of Buccleuch and Queensberry (both in the Peerage of Scotland); the Duke of Argyll, holding one Dukedom of Argyll in the Peerage of Scotland and another in the Peerage of the United Kingdom; and the Duke of Richmond (in the Peerage of England), Lennox and Gordon (both in the Peerage of Scotland). These, with the exception of the Duke of Cornwall, appear only once, in their most senior dukedom.

*2012 * eg York, Kent, Edinburgh, Cornwall, Cambridge (Prince William);*
Prince Andrew - York.
Prince Charles - Cornwall
Prince William - Cambridge

DUKES IN THE PEERAGE

ENGLAND

TITLE	NAME	RESIDENCES
Duke of Norfolk	Fitzalan-Howard	Arundel Castle
		Carlton Towers
Duke of Somerset	Seymour	Bradley House
Duke of Richmond	Gordon-Lennox	Goodwood House
Duke of Grafton	Fitzroy	Euston Hall
Duke of Beaufort	Somerset	Badminton House
Duke of St Albans	de Vere Beauclerk	(not landed)
Duke of Bedford	Russell	Woburn Abbey
Duke of Devonshire	Cavendish	Chatsworth House
		Bolton Abbey
		Lismore Castle
Duke of Marlborough	Spencer-Churchill	Blenheim Palace
Duke of Rutland	Manners	Belvoir Castle

The family pile was sold many years ago. The Duke - Buchan pile in a poor, dearly Regency style terrace house in London. They shall have their coronets & robes.

VICTORIAN WEALTH It was estimated that the minimum sum required to support a gentleman was £1,000 p.a., or the income from 1000 acres. There were about 700 families of this level or above, led by 31 non-Royal dukes. However their was only one heir to each title so younger brothers went into the profession, army or the church, sometimes with a small allowance & frequently DID NOT MARRY. Most heads of family represented old money - only a few ... from business or ...

SCOTLAND

Duke of Hamilton and Brandon	Douglas-Hamilton	Lennoxlove House
Duke of Buccleuch and Queensbury (extremely wealthy)	Montagu-Douglas-Scott	Bowhill House Drumlanrig Castle Boughton House Dalkeith Palace
Duke of Argyll	Campbell	Inveraray Castle
⊕ Duke of Atholl	Murray	Blair Castle
Duke of Montrose (2014 An actual government minister)	Graham	Auchmar House
Duke of Roxburghe	Innes-Ker	Floors Castle

⊕ Atholl - see my notes in Discovering Scottish Castles.

IRELAND

Duke of Leinster	Fitzgerald	-
Duke of Abercorn	Hamilton	Baronscourt

GREAT BRITAIN

Duke of Manchester	Montagu	-
Duke of Northumberland	Percy	Alnwick Castle Syon House

UNITED KINGDOM

Duke of Wellington	Wellesley	Stratfield Saye House Apsley House
Duke of Sutherland	Egerton	Mertoun House
Duke of Westminster*	Grosvenor	Eaton Hall
Duke of Fife	Carnegie	-

* One of the wealthiest in the country. Lots of land (esp. in London) Note Ⓐ

SERVANTS

When Lord North put a tax of one guinea each on male servants in 1772 he estimated that there were about 100,000 male servants (and therefore around 250–300,000 servants in all) in England. The tax was one factor that contributed to female servants predominating as the eighteenth century drew to a close. There was then a population of roughly six million, including children. Having servants did not die out

Ⓐ Duke of Westminster (family Grosvenor) 68th richest in world + 3rd in Britain worth £8bn - died at 64 on Tuesday 9 AUGUST 2016.

until after the Second World War. The Dowager Duchess of Denver calculates (in 1937, in *Busman's Honeymoon*) that Lord Peter Wimsey needed eight servants for himself and his wife 'besides Bunter and the housekeeper'. Any household with the least pretension to gentility kept at least one servant.

In Victorian times a sizeable country house might have accommodated up to 150 people at a time, most of them servants. Further back, in Elizabethan times, several noblemen built country houses solely for the purpose of entertaining the Queen (and her legions of servants). More than one, like Sir Christopher Hatton at Holdenby House, Northants, whom the Queen in fact never visited, went bankrupt.

* On one visit she arrived with over 2000 courtiers.

TITLES AND DUTIES OF MALE SERVANTS

BUTLER or **HOUSE STEWARD.** In charge of the house accounts, the plate chest, the wine cellar, paying wages and hiring servants. His chief concern was keeping the other servants in order.

CHEF or **COOK.** In charge of the kichens.

GROOM OF THE CHAMBERS. Kept the reception rooms and the individual bedrooms in order.

VALET. A gentleman's personal servant.

UNDER BUTLER. Second-in-command to the butler.

FOOTMAN. Originally a servant who walked or ran beside the carriage. In the late seventeenth century, he served in the servants' hall; by the late eighteenth century, he had moved upstairs, standing behind the master's or the mistress's chair. Often given a variety of titles, such as First Footman, Second Footman, or Under Footman.

PANTRY BOY, STABLE BOY. Under-servants who worked in the kitchens and stables.

ODD MAN. A variety of duties, as the name implies. These might include carrying luggage, serving nursery meals, being in charge of the beer cellar and unpacking wines.

COACHMAN. In charge of the stables and of driving the carriages.

GARDENER. Sometimes divided into Head Gardener and Under Gardener. An 'outdoor' servant (like grooms and coachmen) who lived in the stable block. The head gardener was an important man who was treated with respect.

NB A great influence in master/servant relationships was the influential book of 1864 Robert Kerr's "The Gentlemans House" which stated that privacy (separating family from servants) was the most important feature of a property.

GROOM. Attended to and exercised the horses.

TIGER. Sat upright on the box of a carriage and led the ponies of the children of the house. Introduced about 1800.

STEEL BOY. Burnished the metal parts of the harness.

*The name derives from the common uniform of yellow & black stripes

TITLES AND DUTIES OF FEMALE SERVANTS

HOUSEKEEPER. Equal in status to the butler or steward. Made sure the house was clean and kept the housemaids in order.

LADY'S MAID. Attended to her mistress's appearance.

UPPER HOUSEMAID. Lighter jobs such as making beds, tidying bedrooms.

BETWEEN MAID or 'TWEENY'. Worked in the house or kitchen as needed.

LOWER OR UNDER HOUSEMAID. Most of the cleaning and polishing.

HEAD NURSE. In charge of the nurseries.

NURSERY MAID. Subordinate to the nurse.

SEWING MAID. Mending , darning and other needlework.

KITCHEN MAID. General work in the kitchen.

VEGETABLE MAID. Preparation of vegetables.

SCULLERY MAID. Cleaned the kitchen and utensils.

STILL-ROOM MAID. Minor cooking, tea etc.

LAUNDRY MAID. Washing and ironing.

SERVANTS' WAGES

The following section on servants' wages is taken from the *The Book of Household Management,* 1859, by Mrs Isabella Beeton (with all figures converted to modern-day equivalents, rounded to the nearest £1,000):

The following table of the average yearly wages paid to domestics, with the various members of the household placed in the order in which they are usually ranked, will serve as a guide to regulate the expenditure of an establishment:—

Modern Equivalents

MALE SERVANTS	When not found in Livery	When found in Livery
The House Steward	£31–62,000	
The Valet	£20–37,000	£16–23,000
The Butler	£20–37,000	
The Cook	£20–31,000	
The Gardener	£20–31,000	
The Footman	£20–31,000	£12–20,000
The Under Butler	£12–23,000	£12–20,000
The Coachman		£16–27,000
The Groom	£12–23,000	£9–16,000
The Under Footman		£9–16,000
The Page or Footboy	£6–14,000	£5–11,000
The Stableboy	£5–14,000	

→ ie 31000–62000 pa
eg 20,000 = £384 pw
37,000 = £711 pw

FEMALE SERVANTS	When no extra allowance is made for Tea, Sugar, and Beer	When an extra allowance is made for Tea, Sugar, and Beer
The Housekeeper	£15–35,000	£20–31,000
The Lady's-maid	£10–20,000	£8–16,000
The Head Nurse	£12–23,000	£9–20,000
The Cook	£12–23,000	£10–20,000
The Upper Housemaid	£10–16,000	£8–13,000
The Upper Laundry-maid	£9–14,000	£8–12,000
The Maid-of-all-work	£7–9,000	£6–8,000
The Under Housemaid	£6–9,000	£5–8,000
The Still-room Maid	£7–11,000	£6–9,000
The Nursemaid	£6–9,000	£4–8,000
The Under Laundry-maid	£7–11,000	£6–9,000
The Kitchen-maid	£7–11,000	£4–6,000
The Scullery-maid	£4–7,000	£3–6,000

4000 = £76 pw
7000 = £134 pw

These quotations of wages are those usually given in or near the metropolis; but of course, there are many circumstances connected with locality, and also having reference to the long service on the one hand, or the inexperience on the other, of domestics, which may render the wages still higher or lower than those named above. All the domestics mentioned in the above table would enter into the

At Charlecote Warws is a list (in the NT shop) of wages in c1850
Top was Governess £80 p.a
Next Butler £70 pa
Bottom Scullery maid & other basic maids £13 p.a.

establishment of a wealthy nobleman. The number of servants, of course, would become smaller in proportion to the lesser size of the establishment; and we may here enumerate a scale of servants suited to various incomes, commencing with:

About £775,000 a year – A cook, upper housemaid, nursemaid, under housemaid, and a man servant.

About £581,000 a year – A cook, housemaid, nursemaid, and footboy.

About £387,000 a year – A cook, housemaid, and nursemaid.

About £232,000 a year – A maid-of-all-work and nursemaid.

About £155–116,000 a year – A maid-of-all-work (and girl occasionally).

RULES FOR SERVANTS

Never let your voice be heard by the ladies and gentlemen of the household except when necessary, and then as little as possible.

Never begin to talk to your mistress, unless it is to deliver a message, or ask a necessary question. Even then do it as shortly as possible.

Never talk to another servant or person of your own rank, or to a child, in the presence of your mistress, unless from necessity, and then do it as shortly as possible and in a low voice.

Always stand still and keep your hands before you, or at your sides, when you are speaking or being spoken to.

Always stand up when a lady or gentleman comes into the room in which you are.

Should you ever be required to walk with a lady or gentleman, to carry a baby or a parcel, always keep a few paces behind.

Do not smile at droll stories told at table, or seem in any way to notice or enter into the conversation.

Always 'give room': that is, if you encounter one of your betters in the house or on the stairs, you are to make yourself as invisible as possible, turning yourself toward the wall and averting your eyes.

You shall not receive any Relative, Visitor or Friend into the house, nor shall you introduce any person into the Servants' Hall, without the consent of the Butler or Housekeeper.

Followers are strictly forbidden. Any member of the female staff who is found to be fraternizing shall be immediately dismissed.

(*The Servant's Behaviour Book,* by Mrs Motherly, London 1859)

Ⓐ Once the bell system was in use (invented c1780) servants no longer needed to loiter in corridors within earshot of the family. So rules were made about not straying into the families areas, inside or outside, except on business. If seen, servants were told to stand still & look at the floor or even face the wall, and they had to stay away from windows in order not to be seen from outside. Later the speaking tube & telephone replaced the

THE LONDON SEASON

The London Season began, or rose to prominence, in the eighteenth century, when families migrated from the country to London, opened their town houses, and hosted or attended several social events designed to introduce their daughters to eligible bachelors. (At Longleat House, which in Edwardian days had a total of fifty-seven servants, twenty-two staff accompanied the family to London). These social events gradually acquired a framework of public events which, by the turn of the nineteenth and twentieth centuries, had become fixed.

The most important event at the start of the Season was the presentation of unmarried girls (débutantes) to the sovereign at court for the first time. This was 'coming out'. Queen Charlotte (1744–1818, queen of George III) is believed to have begun the practice, which was discontinued in 1958. It took place on two afternoons in May and June, although girls could also be presented at a royal garden party.

The Season began with the Royal Academy's Summer Exhibition, which opened on the first Monday in May, and it closed with sailing at Cowes Week at the beginning of August. It included the Chelsea Flower Show (end of May), the Derby at Ascot (early June), Wimbledon (mid June), the Eton and Harrow match (late June), Henley (beginning of July), and Goodwood (end of July). Afterwards people returned to their country estates for the start of grouse shooting (12 August).

MEALS AND MEAL TIMES

From the fifteenth century, there were three meals a day: breakfast, dinner and supper. Before that, there were only two. Breakfast was frowned upon, except for field labourers or children. In the early nineteenth century, there was a new fashion for luncheon and afternoon tea, meals to fill the gap between breakfast and dinner.

MENU À LA FRANÇAISE

Table covered in all sorts of food & the guests helped themselves though with strict rules.

FIRST COURSE

A piece of beef garnished with pastries, sweetbreads
on skewers, and a reduction of ham
Soups: a pigeon bisque and a capon soup
with lettuce and asparagus tips
Four entrées:
Two fat chickens on skewers with a reduction of ham
Filets mignons with lettuce
Warm baby rabbit paté
Two little goslings with asparagus tips

SECOND COURSE

Three roast dishes:
One of two Campine chickens
One of two hares
One of eight pigeons
Two salads
Two sauces

THIRD COURSE

For the central dish: a ham cooked on a spit
For the two end dishes: a cream tart with little puff pastries
Four between-dishes:
Ham sandwiches
Calves' sweetbreads on skewers with a sauce
Ragoût of mousseron mushrooms
Asparagus in sauce

A *menu à la française* for six to eight diners, copied from Massialot, *Le nouveau cuisinier royal et bourgeois, ou cuisinier moderne* (1748)

MENU À LA RUSSE (Food served in succession modern style from c 1820)

Caviar
Cold appetiser
Soup, clear or thick
Radishes, celery, olives and almonds
Fish
Mushrooms
Artichokes inside a pastry shell
Roast beef
Fruit punch thickened with egg whites
Game with salad
Creamed sweet
Sorbet
Cheeses
Crystallized fruits served with bonbons

A typical *service à la russe* menu

BREAKFAST. From the fifteenth century until the mid-seventeenth century, breakfast consisted of bread, cold meat and small beer. About 1650, chocolate and tea became increasingly common (and coffee a little later), and so did far larger breakfasts. Pepys mentions 'turkey pie and goose, mackerel, pickled oysters, beef, cake and ale, collar of brawn, bread, butter and sweetmeats, cold chine of pork, hashed mutton, dish of cold cream, cream and cakes'. At one house party, in 1779, breakfast was 'an immense table-chocolate-honey-hot bread-cold bread-brown bread-white bread-green bread-and all coloured breads and cakes'. Kedgeree made its appearance in the second half of the nineteenth century. Breakfast in bed became a wealthy habit about 1900.

As in Downton Abbey Breakfast dishes (eggs, bacon, fruit et all) would be served on a large side table. The formerly etc served themselves).

LUNCHEON. Initially, luncheon was an informal meal served at about 3 pm for women only, since the men were out shooting or hunting. Later, the time for luncheon stabilized at around 1 pm. According to Mrs Beeton (*Book of Household Management*, 1861), 'The remains of cold joints, nicely garnished, a few sweets, or a little hashed meat, poultry or game, are the usual articles placed on the table for luncheon, with bread and cheese, biscuits, butter, etc. If a substantial meal is desired, rump-steaks or mutton chops may he served, as also veal cutlets, kidneys, or any dish of that kind.'

AFTERNOON TEA. Taken between 4 pm and 5 pm. This was tea accompanied by sandwiches (cucumber, egg and cress, fish paste, ham, and smoked salmon), scones with clotted cream and jam, and usually cakes and pastries.

DINNER. From late mediaeval times to the mid-nineteenth century, dinner was served according to the *service à la française*. The table was covered with all sorts of food and the guests helped themselves, although following quite strict rules. There were customarily three courses (*services*), with light dishes, heavier dishes and sweets served at each. The choicer dishes were placed before those higher up in the social scale. For the first course, soups, meats, poultry, fish, *hors d'oeuvres* (smaller, lighter dishes) and sweets were served. For the second, heavier dishes of roast meats, fish, vegetables, salads and once more sweets and savouries were served. From about the beginning of the nineteenth century, this course contained the *piéce de résistance*, an elaborate architectural structure of mixed meats or seafoods with various garnishes. For the third course, prepared not in the kitchen but in the pastry, meat patés, cheeses, pastries, fruit and, again, sweets and savouries were served. From about 1820, *service à la russe* came into fashion. This followed the modern fashion, with dishes served in succession, and became universal by about 1860.

SUPPER. This was much more informal meal, comprising bread with cold meat, cheese, soup, salads, and egg and dairy dishes.

MEAL TIMINGS

The time of the main meal, dinner, has got later and later over the centuries. In mediaeval times breakfast was eaten at 6 or 7 am, dinner between 10 and 11 am and supper at 5 pm. By the early eighteenth century, dinner was served between 2 and 3 pm. Fifty years later, it was around 4.30 to 5 pm. By 1840, it was at 7 pm, and by the early years of the twentieth century, it was eaten at 8 pm. Breakfast and supper became correspondingly later. By 1840, breakfast-time had slipped to 10 am or even noon, and supper-time to 10 pm or later.

HORSE-DRAWN CARRIAGES

It was not until the invention of the C–shaped spring in the mid-seventeenth century that carriages became a relatively comfortable, and so an acceptable, form of travel. Previously, men had travelled by horseback and women by horse litters. The elliptical leaf-spring was invented in 1804 by Obadiah Elliott, and, together with 'macadamising' road surfaces (1816), made the construction of smoother, lighter and faster carriages possible. This led to a proliferation of carriage types in the nineteenth century.

BAROUCHE (nineteenth century). Four-wheeled vehicle drawn normally by two horses, but could be drawn by up to six, with a seat in front for the driver and seats inside for two couples to sit facing each other. The body was suspended on C–springs. It had a folding half-hood over the rear seats.

BERLIN (eighteenth century). Four-wheeled travelling carriage. It had two inside seats and a footman's seat, hooded, behind.

BRITCHKA, BRITZKA, BRITSKA (early nineteenth century). Light, two-horse, four-wheeled open carriage, with four seats with a folding top over the rear seat, a driving seat and a rumble seat behind for servants.

BROUGHAM (nineteeth century). Closed, one-horse, two- or four-wheeled, carriage for two or four passengers, with a box-seat in front for driver and servant. Invented (or perhaps simply popularized) in 1839 by Lord Brougham.

BREAK, BRAKE (nineteenth and early twentieth centuries). Large, closed, four-horse, four-wheeled carriage. The shooting break was a large open carriage, with a seat for the driver and footman/gamekeeper, and space for six shooters sitting down the sides.

BUGGY (nineteenth and early twentieth centuries). Light, open, one-horse (on occasion two-horse), two-wheeled vehicle for one or two persons.

CABRIOLET (nineteenth century). Light, one-horse, two-wheeled carriage, with a large hood and an apron. For one or two persons and usually with a platform behind for a servant.

Britska

Canoe Landau

Brougham

Barouche

Clarence Brougham

Four-wheeled Dog Cart

CAB. Abbreviation of 'cabriolet', applied generally to one-horse vehicles, with two or four wheels, for hire. See also **HANSOM CAB**.

CALASH, CALECHE (eighteenth century). Light, small-wheeled, one-horse vehicle for four passengers and a driver, with a removable folding hood.

CARRIOLE, CARIOLE (nineteenth century). Small open or covered carriage, with two or four wheels and one horse, for one person.

CHAISE (eighteenth and nineteenth centuries). Light, fast, two- or four-wheeled vehicle with a folding hood. It was drawn by one horse, sometimes by two, and carried one or two people.

CHARABANC. Long four-wheeled vehicle in which the seats all face forwards.

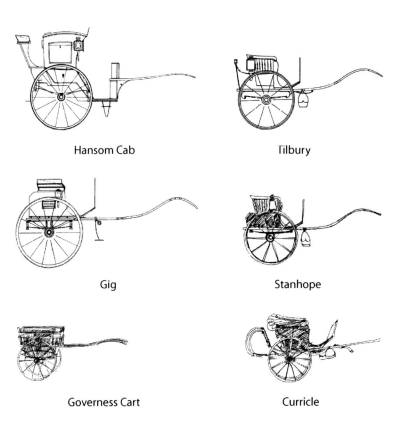

Hansom Cab

Tilbury

Gig

Stanhope

Governess Cart

Curricle

CHARIOT (nineteenth century). Light, four-wheeled carriage, drawn by up to four horses. The driver sat on a coach-box and the passengers behind.

CLARENCE (from about 1840). Closed four-wheeled cab for four passengers, with a window in the front, nicknamed the 'growler' because of the noise made by its steel-rimmed wheels on the cobbles. The driver sat in front. Named for the Duke of Clarence, later William IV.

COACH. Large ceremonial closed four-wheeled vehicle, normally for four passengers with the driver in front, assisted by one or more postillions, and (possibly) footmen behind. But see **STAGECOACH**.

CURRICLE (early nineteenth century). Light, open, two-wheeled vehicle for a driver and passenger, drawn by two horses abreast.

DEMI-LANDAU. See **LANDAULET.**

DILIGENCE. A public stagecoach.

DOG-CART (nineteenth century). An open, one-horse, usually two-wheeled vehicle with two back-to-back benches, one facing forwards and the other backwards. The backwards-facing bench could be shut up to house dogs. A groom sometimes stood on a platform behind.

FLY. Any one-horse light closed vehicle let out for hire.

FOUR-IN-HAND. Four-wheeled, four-horse vehicle driven by one person.

FOUR-WHEELER. Any vehicle, especially a hackney cab, with four wheels.

GIG (nineteenth century). A light, two-wheeled, one-horse carriage.

GOVERNESS-CART, GOVERNESS CAR. Light two-wheeled vehicle with two bench-seats facing each other along the sides.

GROWLER. See **CLARENCE.**

HACKNEY CAB/CARRIAGE/COACH (seventeenth century onwards). Any vehicle that can be hired.

HANSOM, HANSOM CAB (nineteenth century). Light, one-horse, two-wheeled, two-person cab in which the cabby sat in an elevated position behind the passengers. Designed in 1834 by the architect Joseph Aloysius Hansom (1803–82).

JAUNTING-CAR (nineteenth century). Two-wheeled, one-horse vehicle carrying the driver and four persons, two to a side (either back-to-back in the case of an 'outside jaunting car', or face-to-face in an 'inside jaunting car')'

JINGLE. Closed two-wheeled carriage capable of carrying six or eight people with a driver. Used specially in Ireland.

LANDAU (eighteenth and nineteenth centuries). Four-wheeled four-person convertible carriage, drawn by up to six horses, with the roof in two parts. For open driving the front part was completely removed and the rear part folded back. The driver sat on a bench seat and there were normally grooms standing behind.

LANDAULET, DEMI-LANDAU. A small landau.

PHAETON (from mid-eighteenth century). General term for a four-wheeled, one- or two-horse, open carriage with one or two seats facing forwards.

POST-CHAISE (late eighteenth and nineteenth centuries). Four-wheeled, either two- or four-horse, travelling carriage for two to four persons, hired from post-stage to post-stage. The driver generally rode postillion on one of the near horses.

STAGECOACH (late eighteenth and nineteenth centuries). Public four-wheeled coach, usually drawn by four horses and carrying six inside passengers, which operated to a timetable along fixed routes.

STANHOPE (nineteenth century). Light, open, one-horse, one-seated vehicle, originally two-wheeled, later four-wheeled. Named after Hon Henry Fitzroy Stanhope (1787–1864).

TILBURY (nineteenth century). Light open two-wheeled vehicle, for one or two persons, drawn by one horse.

TRAP. See **GIG**.

VICTORIA (second half of nineteenth century). Low, light, four-wheeled carriage, drawn by one or two horses, with two forward-facing seats, a collapsible top, and a raised driving seat. Named after Queen Victoria.

WAGONETTE (second half of nineteenth century). Four-wheeled vehicle, usually two-horses, carrying from six to eight passengers on inward-facing seats, with one or two seats facing forwards. Either open or with a removable cover.

WHISKY (nineteenth century). Two-wheeled, one-horse vehicle for one or two persons.

MUSICAL INSTRUMENTS

Most collections of musical instruments are in museums: the Victoria and Albert, the Ashmolean and, especially, the Bate Collection in Oxford, which has over 2,000 instruments. Visitors to country houses are unlikely to see examples of many of these instruments: they are much more likely to see them in pictures, wood carvings or sculptures. There are, however, small collections of keyboard instruments in country houses. Fenton House, Hampstead, London (c.1686, this was in the country at the time) has nineteen instruments; Finchcocks, Goudhurst, Kent (1725) has over a hundred; and Hatchlands

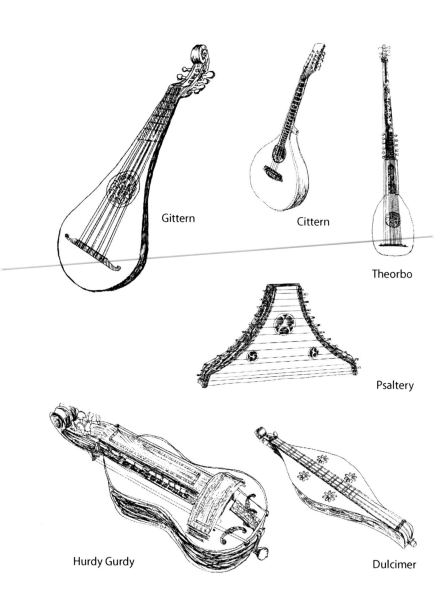

Gittern

Cittern

Theorbo

Psaltery

Hurdy Gurdy

Dulcimer

Park, Guildford, Surrey (1750s) has about fifty. Snowshill Manor, Glos (c.1600) has a room devoted to a substantial collection of old instruments, many of them not listed here.

KEYBOARD

CHAMBER ORGAN. Small organ with one or two keyboards.

CLAVICHORD. Small keyboard instrument, developed in the sixteenth century, in which a metal blade strikes the string when a key is pressed. Superseded in the eighteenth century by the fortepiano.

DULCE MELOS (Latin 'sweet melody'). Predecessor of the harpsichord from the fourteenth to the seventeenth centuries.

FORTEPIANO. Early form of piano, invented by Cristofori in 1709, which had small leather-bound hammers.

HARPSICHORD. Eighteenth-century keyboard instrument. When the keys are pressed the strings are plucked by a leather or quill jack, rather than struck with a hammer as in a piano. Also called cembalo, clavicembalo and clavecin.

HARMONIUM. Small organ invented in about 1842 by Alexandre Debain in France. Air produced by foot-operated bellows created an airflow which caused thin metal tongues to vibrate when a key was pressed.

PORTATIVE ORGAN. Very small mediaeval and Renaissance organ with one keyboard and one range of pipes. It could be carried over the shoulder by a strap.

SPINET. Precursor of the harpsichord. It was developed in the seventeenth century, and had single strings and a range of three and a half octaves.

VIRGINALS. Keyboard instrument of the sixteenth and seventeenth centuries, similar to the harpsichord and spinet except that the strings are at right angles to the keyboard.

STRINGS

ARCHLUTE. See **THEORBO.**

CITTERN. Developed about 1500 and superseded in the nineteenth century by the guitar. It had four pairs of strings and was plucked with the fingers.

DULCIMER. Early form of the zither, which spread to Europe from the Middle East about 1100. It has shallow open soundbox with strings stretched above it. The strings are struck with hammers or beaters.

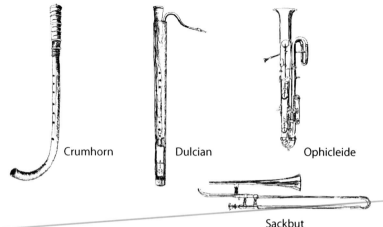

Crumhorn   Dulcian   Ophicleide

Sackbut

GAMBA. See VIOL.

GITTERN. Early four- or five-stringed form of guitar played with a plectrum. It died out in about 1400, but in the sixteenth and seventeenth centuries its name was applied to other members of the guitar family.

HURDY GURDY. Six-stringed instrument in which only the top string is played by a kind of keyboard, while a wheel, operated by a handle, makes the other strings play a drone.

LUTE. Pear-shaped instrument with up to seven strings (single or double), played by plucking with the fingers.

LYRA/LERO/LEERO VIOL or VIOL LYRA WAY. A small bass viol, in use c.1650–1700.

LYRE. Ancient four- to ten-stringed instrument played resting on the knees with the fingers or a plectrum.

MANDOLIN. Almond-shaped instrument with four to six double strings and a fretted fingerboard, played by plucking with the fingers.

PSALTERY. Triangular instrument, with the point at the top and strung laterally. It could be played with a plectrum, fingers, or a bow. It became obsolete during the seventeenth century.

REBEC or REBECK. Instrument of Arab origin with three strings and played with a bow. It lingered on until the eighteenth century as a street instrument.

THEORBO or ARCHLUTE. Bass lute, common c.1500–1700, which has two sets of strings on one neck. The shorter, or bass, strings are plucked by the thumb, and the longer five to seven strings are plucked by the fingers. It has a fretted fingerboard.

VIOL. Treble, tenor and bass. Predecessor of the violin family, common in England 1540–1700. Six-stringed, with fretted fingerboards, they were played upright, resting on the leg (*da gamba*) or knee. A chest of viols was a cupboard or chest containing a set of (usually) six viols of various sizes.

VIOLA D'AMORE. Common 1600–1750. A member of the viol family, but played under the chin, without a fretted fingerboard, and had seven bowed strings and seven sympathetic strings (which are sounded by resonance from the bowed strings). Similar to the *violin d'amour*, which had five bowed strings and six sympathetic strings.

WOODWIND

CHALUMEAU (pl. chalumeaux). Reeded instrument, late seventeenth and eighteenth centuries, developed from the recorder, which it much resembles. It has a large eighteenth-century repertoire. Gave way to the clarinet.

CRUMHORN. Fifteenth-century double-reeded instrument, with the double reeds enclosed in a windcap (a cap preventing the player's lips from touching the reeds). It looks like a walking stick and is blown through the ferrule end.

DULCIAN or **CURTAL.** Sixteenth-century double-reeded instrument, ancestor of the bassoon.

OBOE D'AMORE or **OBOE DA CACCIA** (Italian, 'hunting oboe'). Earlier (two keys), and lower (minor third and a fifth lower), versions of the oboe.

SERPENT. Sixteenth to nineteenth century S–shaped, or double S–shaped, tubular brass or wooden keyed instrument.

SHAWM. Double-reeded instrument with a windcap and fingerholes. It was a forerunner of the oboe developed in the thirteenth century.

BRASS

CORNETT. Precursor of the trumpet.

NATURAL HORN. Forerunner of the French horn, which it resembles. It has no valves.

OPHICLEIDE. A conical brass tube bent double, with (usually) eleven keys.

SACKBUT. Predecessor of the trombone from the fourteenth century until the nineteenth.

PERCUSSION

TABOR. Small drum used to accompany a fife or recorder.

TIMBREL. Early form of the tambourine.

DANCES

COTILLION. Family of dances popular from the late eighteenth century, until replaced by the quadrille. For four couples, the cotillion consisted of a 'figure' (chorus, different for each cotillion) and nine 'changes', danced between each figure.

DANSE BASSE. A quiet, graceful dance originating in Burgundy in the fifteenth century.

GALLIARD. A quick and lively dance in 3/4 time.

GAVOTTE. A kind of minuet but more lively.

LANDLER. A hopping and stamping dance popular at the end of the eighteenth century, later made quicker and more elegant. Forerunner of the waltz.

LANCERS. A later version of the quadrille, introduced in 1836.

MAZURKA. A lively Polish dance resembling the polka. In 3/4 time.

MINUET. A slow, stately dance in 3/4 time for two persons. Fashionable throughout the eighteenth century.

PAVANE. A grave and stately dance in 2/2 time, introduced into England in the sixteenth century.

POLKA. Lively dance of Bohemian origin, first brought to England in 1842. In 2/4 time.

QUADRILLE. Square dance usually performed by four couples and consisting of five sets, each being complete within itself. Introduced into England about 1820.

WALTZ. Originally a peasant dance, it burst upon the civilized world—a 'riotous and indecent' dance—at the end of the eighteenth century. It was riotous and indecent because the gentleman clasped the lady close to him. In 3/4 time.

OTHER PASTIMES

Time must have hung heavy on the hands of the country house dweller or his guest, what with servants to cater for his every need. It is not surprising therefore that the day was passed in outdoor pursuits when fine, and indoor ones when wet. All the pastimes listed here still exist although sometimes in a slightly different form. Foxhunting is the exception: it has been illegal in Scotland since 2002 and in England and Wales since 2004, although it is not yet so in Northern Ireland.

The foxhunts now are supposed to use artificial lures but one sometimes find to chase real foxes (a mistake they usually claim). The anti-hunting lobby keep an eye on them often with confrontations.

AMATEUR DRAMATICS. Came into fashion in the mid-eighteenth century. Previously acting had been regarded as rather lower class. Among early 'productions' were *Jane Shore* and *The fair penitent* by Nicholas Rowe, the former put on at Holland House, London in 1761 and the latter at Seaton Delaval Hall, Northumb, in 1790. Amateur dramatics take place in Jane Austen (*Mansfield Park*, 1814), with a stage created in the billiard room. Charles Dickens was famous for his love of acting and producing, in town and in country houses.

BILLIARDS. There was a billiard table in the Staircase Hall at Belton House, Lincs, in 1688 and a seventeenth century table still exists, with its maces (curved cues), in the Leicester Gallery at Knole Park. Billiards became popular in the late eighteenth century and tables were set up in the hall. Country houses built in the nineteenth century nearly always contained a billiard room, normally next to the smoking room.

BOARD GAMES. The three most important (and most long-lived) board games were draughts, chess and backgammon. Draughts in its modern form was developed in France in about 1535 and came to England around 1600. Chess had been popular since the fifteenth century and backgammon ('the tables') since the sixteenth.

Backgammon fell temporarily out of fashion towards the end of the eighteenth century but was revived in the 1920s.

CARDS. Since at least the sixteenth century, the most popular of indoor pastimes. Many early card games have died out, such as ombre (seventeenth century) and loo (1660s). Some, despite their early origin, are still played, such as piquet (arriving in England 1550s), cribbage (early seventeenth century) and whist (seventeenth century). Some are more modern: écarté (nineteenth century), patience (or solitaire: second half of the nineteenth century) and bridge (1890s). Gambling at cards was disapproved of but still took place at country houses: baccarat (sixteenth century), vingt et un (also blackjack, perhaps seventeenth century) and faro (eighteenth century).

DRAWING AND PAINTING. In the eighteenth and nineteenth centuries, young ladies were encouraged to learn drawing and painting in watercolours, and country houses are full of albums of their work. Some attempted to paint in oils, and a few were successful, such as Rebecca Dulcibella Orpen (1845–1923). Drawing and painting as part of a young lady's education seems to have died out in the early twentieth century.

FISHING. Like hunting and hawking, fishing has a very long history, and similarly emerged into the modern world in the seventeenth century, with the publication of Isaac Walton's *Compleat Angler* in 1653. (The very first book on angling, The *Treatyse on Fysshynge with an Angle*, by Dame Juliana Berners, was published in 1496). The 'fishing house' was heard of in the sixteenth century but became popular in the mid-eighteenth. Fishing continued to develop in the nineteenth and twentieth centuries—although not as a country house pursuit—and is now said to be the largest participative sport in Britain.

HAWKING. Ancient sport of kings and the higher aristocracy until King John's time (1199–1216), when all freemen were permitted to hawk. It began to decline in the seventeenth century with the development of better firearms, and by the end of the century had more or less died out.

HUNTING. The last boar was killed in Britain in 1683 and stag hunting retreated to the country's wild areas, leaving fox hunting the sole pursuit. The first pack of foxhounds was bred by Lord Arundel between 1690 and 1700. Hunts are largely the creation of the eighteenth century, but grew enormously in the nineteenth. The season ran from November to April, with cubbing (the hunting of young foxes) in September.

NEEDLEWORK. Decorative needlework was a standard pursuit of women and girls of the leisured classes, and the golden age of embroidery was in the seventeenth and eighteenth centuries. It declined in the nineteenth, the first embroidery machine having been invented in 1828 and the first sewing machine in 1851.

SHOOTING. Modern shooting developed at the turn of the eighteenth and nineteenth centuries. Breech loading became common in the early 1800s, and the self-contained cartridge was invented in Paris in 1808. Game licences, compulsory for those who kept game on their land, were introduced in 1784. The Game Act of 1831 made illegal the shooting of game during the breeding season, and introduced licences to sell game. During the nineteenth century, shooting became highly organized. The pheasant to some extent replaced the partridge, driving over standing guns was introduced, planting of covers developed, and the battue (competition to kill the largest number of birds) became common.

Grouse was/is shot on moors esp. in the Highlands, usually over standing guns with beaters driving the birds out to fly across the shooters. Still done (but frowned on) by the Royals when at Balmoral. Nowadays numbers shot are much controlled, the birds supplying local or not so local game butchers... Nowadays deer herds are only shot, by marksmen specially licenced for culling purposes.

Prince Edward (Victoria's wayward son) made Sandringham a great shooting venue - he purchased an extra 7000 acres of land and had it planted specifically for shooting. The season began on Nov 9th (on Bertie's birthday) and he entertained all manner of the great & good (or not so great or good), including the Tsar of Russia and Kaiser Wilhelm. On one day's single shoot 1300 partridge were accounted for. Edward even had the clocks on the estate forwarded one hour to give more daylight for the shoot. A more problematic shooting was of wildfowl and, in fact, on the coast were made the first attempts to preserve wildfowl/birds as numbers were fast declining. So a society to protect the wildfowl was started and, amazingly, Edward became its president !!! The reared birds still got shot of course !

COUNTRY HOUSES, WHAT ARE THEY NOW?

Below are listed the status and present ownership of all country houses (and some related buildings) mentioned in this book.

A considerable number of country houses are divided into apartments, or have become schools or hotels or conference centres. One is a prison and one an army headquarters. Surprisingly few country houses are still private residences. Those that are, are mostly also generating income as tourist attractions, wedding or event venues, or up-market bed and breakfasts. Country houses that are still used as residences, and nothing more, seem to be quite scarce.

Where there is documentary evidence of the fact that a house is not open to the public, this has been stated in the entry. Otherwise, all buildings should, in theory, be visitable.

Ownership is more complicated. Chatsworth is not owned by the Duke of Devonshire but by the Chatsworth House Trust; many more country houses are owned by trusts. So are most of those that have become schools, colleges, museums and nursing homes. Hotels are mostly owned by limited companies. Country houses which have been divided into residences may have sold the residences freehold or leasehold. Even the National Trust is not straightforward; some properties are rented, with consequent limitations on visiting. Cronkhill, for example, is only open for four days a year. For country houses which are still private residences, the name of the owner is only given where the owner's name is reasonably well-known. For some country houses it has not been possible to determine current ownership. These are listed as 'ownership at present unknown'.

A

Abbotsford, Borders	The Abbotsford Trust
Adcote, Salop	School
Airthrey Castle, Stirling	Part of the University of Stirling
Alderley House, Glos	School
Alkerton Grange, Glos	Ownership at present unknown
Alkrington Hall, Lancs	Divided into three residences
Allestree Hall, Derbys	Derby City Council, mostly unoccupied

Alnwick Castle, Northumb	Duke of Northumberland
Alscot Park, Warwicks	Privately owned
Althorp, Northants	Earl Spencer
Alton Castle, Staffs	Archdiocese of Birmingham, Catholic Youth Retreat Centre
Alton Towers, Staffs	Merlin Entertainments, partly ruinous
Amesbury Abbey, Wilts	Nursing home
Ampthill Park House, Beds	Divided into four residences
Anglesey Abbey, Cambs	National Trust
Arbury Hall, Warwicks	Privately owned
Arniston House, Midlothian	Privately owned
Arundel Castle, Sussex	Duke of Norfolk
Asgill House, Surrey	Privately owned
Ashburnham Place, Sussex	Largely demolished, remains being a Christian conference centre
Ashdown House, Berks	National Trust
Ashridge House, Herts	Management college
Aske Hall, N. Yorks	Marquess of Zetland
Aston Hall, W. Mid	Birmingham City Council, museum
Aston Hall, Salop	Privately owned
Attingham Park, Salop	National Trust
Aubrey House, London	Privately owned
Auchmar House, Stirling	Duke of Montrose
Audley End, Essex	English Heritage
Avery Hill, London	Partly destroyed by fire, remains are part of the University of London
Aynhoe Park, Oxon	Privately owned
Ayscoughfee Hall, Lincs	South Holland District Council, now a museum

B

Badminton House, Glos (Cirencester)	Duke of Beaufort, not open to the public { Famous Big Ground
Baldersby Park, N. Yorks	Formerly Newby Park, now Queen Mary's School
Ballyfin, Co. Leix	Ownership at present unknown
Balmoral, Aberdeenshire	Royal palace
Baronscourt, Co. Tyrone	Duke of Abercorn
Barrington Court, Som	National Trust
Battlesden House, Beds	Mostly demolished in 1866
Bearforest, Co. Cork	Ownership at present unknown
Bellamont House, Co. Cavan	Ownership at present unknown, for sale 2010

Belmont House, Kent	Privately owned
Belton House, Lincs	National Trust
Belvoir Castle, Rut	Duke of Rutland
Benfleet Hall, Surrey	Residences
Beningbrough Hall, N. Yorks	National Trust
Berrington Hall, Herefs	National Trust
Bilton Grange, Warwicks	School
Blair Castle, Perth and Kinross	Duke of Atholl
Blenheim Palace, Oxon	Duke of Marlborough
Blickling Hall, Norfolk	National Trust
Bodnant Garden, Conwy	National Trust
Bodnant House, Conwy	Privately owned
Bodrhyddan Hall, Flints	Baron Langford, wedding venue
Bolsover Castle, Derbys	English Heritage
Bolton Abbey, N. Yorks	Duke of Devonshire
Boothby Pagnell Hall, Lincs	Ownership at present unknown
Borris House, Co. Carlow	Privately owned, wedding venue
Boughton House, Northants	Duke of Buccleuch and Queensbury
Bourton Manor, Salop	Privately owned, self-catering accommodation
Bowhill House, Borders	Duke of Buccleuch and Queensbury
Bowood House, Wilts	Marquis of Lansdowne, largely demolished 1955
Bradley House, Wilts	Duke of Somerset, wedding and corporate events venue
Bramham Park, W. Yorks	Privately owned
Bramshott Grange, Hants	Demolished 1990s
Brandsby Hall, N. Yorks	Ownership at present unknown
Brasted Place, Kent	Apartments
Broad Leys, Cumb	HQ of the Windermere Motor Boat Club
Broadlands, Hants	Privately owned, reopening to the public in July 2012
Broadway Tower, Warwicks	Privately owned {now holiday apartments}
Brocklesby Park, Lincs	Earl of Yarborough
Brodsworth Hall, S. Yorks	English Heritage
Brunstane House, Midlothian	Ownership at present unknown
Bryanston House, Dorset	Bryanston School
Buckland House, Oxon	Privately owned
Burghley House, Lincs	Burghley House Preservation Trust
Burley-on-the-Hill House, Rut	Apartments
Burton Agnes Hall, E. Yorks	Burton Agnes Preservation Trust
Burton Constable Hall, E. Yorks	Burton Constable Foundation

C

Caerhays Castle, Cornwall	Privately owned, corporate and holiday facilities
Caldwell House, Ayrshire	Roofless, interior largely destroyed Ownership at present unknown
Calke Abbey, Derbys	National Trust
Camden House, Glos	Burnt 1640s, but banqueting halls survive, conserved by the Landmark Trust
Camden Place, Kent	Chiselhurst Golf Club House
Canford Manor, Dorset	School
Cannon Hall, S. Yorks	Barnsley Council, museum and regimental museum
Cannons, London	Burned 1747
Carlton House, London	Demolished 1825
Carlton Towers, N. Yorks	Duke of Norfolk, wedding venue
Carshalton House, Surrey	Now part of St Philomena's High School for Girls
Cashel Palace, Co. Tipperary	Hotel
Cassiobury Park, Herts	Demolished 1927
Castle Bromwich Hall, W. Mid	Sold 2009, present ownership unknown, not open to the public ${ Hotel run by chinese, gardens open to public
Castle Coole, Co. Fermanagh	National Trust
Castle Drogo, Devon	National Trust
Castle Howard, N. Yorks	Privately owned
Castle Mona, Isle of Man	Hotel
Castle Ward, Co. Down	National Trust
Castlegar, Co. Galway	Ownership at present unknown
Castletown House, Co. Kildare	Office of Public Works, Ireland
Charlecote Park, Warwicks	National Trust
Charlton House, London	London Borough Council, community centre and wedding venue
Chastleton House, Oxon	National Trust
Chateau, The, Gate Burton, Lincs	Privately owned, managed by The Landmark Trust
Chatelherault, Lanarkshire	Lanarkshire Council
Chatsworth House, Derbys	Chatsworth House Trust
Chestal House, Glos	Ownership at present unknown
Chesters House, Northumb	Ownership at present unknown
Chettle House, Dorset	Privately owned, wedding venue
Chicheley Hall, Bucks	Conference centre
Chillington Hall, Staffs	Privately owned, wedding and conference venue

Chirk Castle, Den	National Trust
Chiswick House, London	English Heritage
Clandon Park, Surrey	National Trust
Claremont House, Surrey	School, National Trust owns part of the grounds
Clarendon House, London	Demolished 1683
Claverton Manor, Som	The American Museum in Britain
Claydon House, Bucks	National Trust
Clearwell Castle, Glos	Ownership at present unknown Wedding venue
Cliveden House, Bucks	National Trust, leased as an hotel
Clontarf Castle, Co. Dublin	Hotel
Clouds House, Wilts	Nursing home
Cloverley Hall, Salop	Cloverley Hall Ltd., Christian conference centre
Cobham Hall, Kent	School
Coleby Hall, Lincs	Privately owned, divided into three houses, with the outbuildings converted to five more. Not open to the public
Coleorton Hall, Leics	Apartments
Coleshill, Berks	Demolished 1952
Compton Place, Sussex	Language school
Compton Verney, Warwicks	Art gallery
Condover Hall, Salop	Residential activity centre
Constable Burton Hall, N. Yorks	Privately owned, not open to the public
Coombe Abbey, Warwicks	Hotel _Adjacent Country Park_
Cornbury Park, Oxon	Privately owned, Lord and Lady Rotherwick
Corsham Court, Wilts	Privately owned
Cotehele House, Cornwall	National Trust
Cothay Manor, Som	Privately owned
Cottesbrooke Hall, Northants	Privately owned
Cragside, Northumb	National Trust (_formerly Lord Armstrong full of mod. cons._)
Craighall Castle, Perth and Kinross	Ownership at present unknown
Craigiehall House, West Lothian	HQ, 2nd Division, British Army
Cranage Hall, Ches	Hotel
Cranbury Park, Hants	Privately owned, house not generally open to the public
Crichel House, Dorset	Privately owned
Cronkhill, Salop	National Trust
Crooksbury, Surrey	Divided into residences

Croome Court, Worcs	National Trust
Croxteth Hall, Lancs	Liverpool City Council
Culzean Castle, Ayrshire	National Trust for Scotland
Cumbernauld House, Dunbartonshire	CHB Developments Ltd., for sale 2010

D

Dalemain, Cumb	Privately owned
Dalkeith Palace, Midlothian	Duke of Buccleuch and Queensbury, leased to the University of Wisconsin
Dalmahoy House, Midlothian	Hotel
Dalmeny House, West Lothian	Earl of Rosebery
Danbury Place, Essex	Ownership at present unknown, planning permission granted (May 2006) for apartments
Danny House, Sussex	Privately owned, retirement accommodation
Danson House, London	English Heritage
Dartrey House, Co. Monaghan	Demolished, but the stable block survives
Davenport House, Salop	Privately owned, wedding and conference venue
Daylesford House, Glos	Sir Anthony and Lady Bamford, gardens but not house open to the public
Deanery, The, Berks	Privately owned, not open to the public
Deene Park, Northants	Privately owned, seat of the Brudenell family
Dingley Hall, Northants	Seven houses and three flats
Dinton House, Wilts	See Philipps House, Wilts
Ditchley Park, Oxon	Ditchley Foundation, international conference centre
Doddington Hall, Lincs	Privately owned, wedding venue
Dodington Park, Glos	Privately owned by James Dyson
Dorton House, Kent	School for the blind
Downhill, Co. Derry	National Trust, the house is destroyed but the Mussenden Temple survives
Dowsby Hall, Lincs	Privately owned
Drayton House, Northants	Privately owned, not open to the public but can be visited by groups with a prior written appointment
Drum, The, Midlothian	Ownership at present unknown

Drumcondra House, Co. Dublin	University college
Drumlanrig Castle, Dumfries and Galloway	Duke of Buccleuch and Queensbury
Drummond Castle, Perth and Kinross	Grimsthorpe and Drummond Castle Trust, the gardens are open to the public but not the castle
Duddingston House, Midlothian	Headquarters of several companies
Duff House, Moray	Historic Scotland, National Galleries of Scotland and Aberdeenshire Council, gallery and wedding
Dumfries House, Ayrshire	Owned since 2007 by Great Steward of Scotland's Dumfries House Trust, a consortium formed by the Scottish Government and various heritage charities
Duncombe Park, N. Yorks	Privately owned, wedding venue. Gutted by fire in 1879 but restored
Dunham Massey Hall, Ches	National Trust
Dunmore House, Stirling	Ruinous, ownership at present unknown
Dyrham Park, Glos	National Trust

E

Eastnor Castle, Herefs	Privately owned
Easton Neston, Northants	Privately owned, not open to the public
Eaton Hall, Ches	Duke of Westminster, not normally open to the public
Edgcote House, Oxon	Privately owned
Elemore Hall, Durham	School
Elvaston Hall, Derbys	Derbyshire County Council
Erddig Hall, Denbighshire	National Trust
Euston Hall, Suffolk	Duke of Grafton
Exton Park, Leics	Family seat of the Noels, not normally open to the public

F

Fairlawne, Kent	Privately owned, Prince Khalid bin Abdullah
Falkland House, Fife	Special needs school
Farnborough Hall, Warwicks	National Trust
Felbrigg Hall, Norfolk	National Trust
Fenton House, London	National Trust

Fetcham Park, Surrey	Office accommodation
Ffynone, Pembs	Earl Lloyd George
Finchcocks, Kent	Privately owned
Firle Place, Sussex	Viscount Gage
Floors Castle, Borders	Duke of Roxburghe
Folly Farm, Berks	Privately owned, not open to the public
Fonthill Abbey, Wilts	Collapsed and demolished c.1845, extant gatehouse is now privately owned
Fota Island, Co. Cork	Irish Heritage Trust
Frampton Court, Glos	Family seat of the Cliffords, now an up-market bed and breakfast
Fulbrook House, Surrey	Ownership at present unknown

G

Gibside, Tyne & W.	National Trust
Gilling Castle, N. Yorks	St Martin's, Ampleforth, a prep school for Ampleforth College
Glen Andred, Sussex	Ownership at present unknown
Glenarm Castle, Co. Antrim	Viscount Dunluce
Glendoick, Perth and Kinross	Ownership at present unknown
Glevering Hall, Suffolk	Privately owned
Golden Grove, Carms	Ownership at present unknown
Goodwood House, Sussex	Earl of March, wedding and conference venue
Gorhambury House, Herts	Earl of Verulam
Gosfield Hall, Essex	Company-owned wedding venue
Gosford Castle, Co. Armagh	Apartments
Gracefield Lodge, Co. Kildare	Ownership at present unknown
Gravetye Manor, Sussex	Saphos Hotels
Great Chalfield Manor, Wilts	National Trust
Grimsthorpe Castle, Lincs	Baroness Willoughby de Eresby

H

Haddo House, Aberdeenshire	National Trust for Scotland
Haddon Hall, Derbys	Duke of Rutland
Hagley Hall, Worcs	Viscount Cobham
Hall Barn, Bucks	Privately owned, not open to the public
Ham House, Surrey	National Trust
Hamilton Palace, Lanarkshire	Demolished 1921
Hampton Court House, Surrey	School
Hampton Court Palace, London	Royal palace
Hanbury Hall, Worcs	National Trust

Hardwick Hall, Durham	Hotel
Hardwick Hall, Derbys	National Trust
Harewood House, W. Yorks	Harewood House Trust, visitor attraction
Harlaxton Manor, Lincs	British Campus of the University of Evansville, Indiana, USA
Hartwell House, Bucks	Spa hotel
Hatchlands Park, Surrey	National Trust
Hatfield House, Herts	Marquess of Salisbury
Hatley Park, Cambs	Ownership at present unknown
Hawarden Castle, Flintshire	Charles Gladstone, not open to the public
Hawford, Worcs	National Trust
Heathcote, W. Yorks	Ownership at present unknown, for sale October 2010
Heaton Hall, Lancs	Manchester City Council, museum and events venue
Hengrave Hall, Suffolk	Privately owned, wedding and functions venue
Heveningham Hall, Suffolk	Privately owned
Hever Castle, Kent	Broadland Properties Ltd., conference centre and tourist attraction
Heythrop Park, Oxon	Hotel and country club
Hidcote Manor, Glos	National Trust
Highclere Castle, Hants	Earl of Carnarvon, private and corporate events
Hill House, Argyll and Bute	National Trust for Scotland
Holdenby House, Northants	Privately owned, not open to the public
Holkham Hall, Norfolk	Earl of Leicester
Hollybrook House, Co. Wicklow	Partly destroyed by fire in 1969, now five dwellings
Homewood, Herts	Privately owned and until recently an up-market bed and breakfast
Honington Hall, Warwicks	Privately owned, not generally open to the public but may be visited by groups by prior arrangement
Hopetoun House, West Lothian	Marquess of Linlithgow
Horseheath, Cambs	Demolished 1792
Horsted Place, Sussex	Hotel
Horton Tower, Dorset	Vodafone, wooden interior rotted away
Houghton Hall, Norfolk	Marquess of Cholmondeley

I

Ickworth House, Suffolk	National Trust
Inveraray Castle, Argyll and Bute	Duke of Argyll

K

Kedleston Hall, Derbys	National Trust
Kelham Hall, Notts	Head office of Newark and Sherwood District Council
Kelmscott Manor, Oxon	Society of Antiquaries, London
Ken Hill, Norfolk	Ownership at present unknown
Kensington Palace, London	Royal palace
Kenwood House, London	English Heritage
Kew Palace, Surrey	Royal palace
Kidbrooke Park, Sussex	School and wedding venue
Killerton House, Devon	National Trust
Killymoon Castle, Co. Tyrone	Privately owned, visit to the castle can be made by prior appointment
Kilnwick House, E. Yorks	Mostly demolished 1951, ownership at present unknown
Kimbolton Castle, Cambs	School
Kings Weston House, Bristol	Privately owned business and conference centre
Kingston Lacy, Dorset	National Trust
Kinlet Hall, Salop	School
Kinmel Hall, Den	Derbyshire Investments (2010)
Kinross House, Perth and Kinross	Ownership at present unknown, planning permission for a hotel granted.
Kinwarton Dovecote	National Trust
Kirby Hall, Northants	Earl of Winchilsea, semi-ruinous
Kirkleatham Hall, N. Yorks	Demolished 1954
Kirtlington Park, Oxon	Privately owned, wedding venue
Kiveton Hall, W. Yorks	Demolished 1812
Knole Park, Kent	National Trust
Knowsley Hall, Lancs	Earl of Derby, conference, corporate events and wedding centre

L

Lacock Abbey, Wilts	National Trust
Lamport Hall, Northants	Lamport Hall Preservation Trust
Langley Hall, Norfolk	School
Langleys, Essex	Privately owned, not open to the public

Lanhydrock, Cornwall	National Trust
Lasborough Park, Glos	Ownership at present unknown
Lawers House, Perth and Kinross	Ownership at present unknown
Leigh Court, Som	Conference venue
Lennoxlove House, East Lothian	Duke of Hamilton.
Leonardslee House, Sussex	Private ownership, not open to the public
Lethington House, East Lothian	See Lennoxlove
Letterfourie House, Moray	Ownership at present unknown, for sale September 2010
Letton Hall, Norfolk	Christian conference centre
Levens Hall, Cumb	Privately owned
Leys Wood, Sussex	Mostly destroyed, ownership at present unknown
Lilleshall Hall, Staffs	Part of a National Sports Centre
Linley Hall, Salop	Privately owned
Lismore Castle, Co. Waterford	Duke of Devonshire
Little Moreton Hall, Ches	National Trust
Little Thakeham, Sussex	Privately owned
Longford Castle, Wilts	Earl of Radnor
Longleat House, Wilts	Marquess of Bath, safari park and many other attractions
Longner Hall, Salop	Privately owned
Lough Cutra Castle, Co. Galway	Privately owned, wedding venue and private parties
Loughton Hall, Essex	Care home
Lowther Castle, Cumbria	Contents removed late 1940s, roof removed 1957, ownership at present unknown
Lumley Castle, Durham	Hotel
Luscombe Castle, Devon	Privately owned
Lyme Park, Ches	National Trust
Lypiatt Park, Glos	Privately owned { formerly Princess Pushy & husband · Prince & Princess Michael of Kent, now moved into their new home in London }
M	
Mamhead Park, Devon	Rockeagle Securities Ltd., home of several companies
Margam Castle, Glam	Neath Port Talbot County Borough Council
Melbourne Hall, Derbys	Lord and Lady Kerr { formerly Viscount Melbourne
Melbury House, Dorset	Family seat of the Strangways family
Mellerstain House, Borders	Earl of Haddington, weddings, corporate events and private parties

Menagerie, The, Northants	Privately owned, not open to the public but may be visited by groups by prior appointment
Mentmore Towers, Bucks	Mentmore Towers Ltd. (i.e. privately owned). There are plans to turn it into an hotel
Mereworth Castle, Kent	Privately owned, Mr Mahdi al-Tajir, not open to the public
Mersham-le-Hatch, Kent	Privately owned, family seat of the Knatchbulls, not open to the public
Mertoun House, Borders	Duke of Sutherland
Middleton Lodge, N. Yorks	Privately owned, wedding venue, corporate conferences and special events
Millichope Park, Salop	Privately owned, not open to the public
Milton Abbey House, Dorset	School
Milton Hall, Cambs	Seat of the Fitzwilliam family, not open to the public
Moggerhanger House, Beds	Moggerhanger House Preservation Trust, home to several charities and conference and training centre
Montacute House, Som	National Trust
Moor Crag, Cumb	Ownership at present unknown
Moor Park, Herts	Golf club
Moulsham Hall, Essex	Demolished 1809
Mount Stewart, Co. Down	National Trust
Munstead Wood, Surrey	Ownership at present unknown
Murdoustoun Castle, Lanarkshire	Four Seasons Health Care, care home

N

Nashdom, Bucks	Apartments
New Hall, Essex	Largely demolished 1737, now a school
New Wardour Castle, Wilts	Apartments
Newburgh Priory, N. Yorks	Privately owned, Sir George and Lady Wombwell
Newby Hall, N. Yorks	Privately owned
Newby Park	See Baldersby Park
Normanby Hall, Lincs	North Lincolnshire Council
Norris Castle, IoW	Privately owned, not open to the public
Northington Grange, Hants	English Heritage
Nostell Priory, W. Yorks	National Trust
Nuneham Park, Oxon	Retreat centre
Nunnington Hall, N. Yorks	National Trust

Nuthall Temple, Notts	Demolished 1929
Nymans, Sussex	National Trust

O

Oatlands Park, Surrey	Demolished 1649, new hotel now on site
Octagon House, Middx	Art gallery
Okeover Hall, Staffs	Privately owned, family seat of the Okeovers, not open to the public
Orchard, The, Herts	Ownership at present unknown
Orchards, Surrey	Privately owned
Ormesby Hall, N. Yorks	National Trust
Osberton House, Notts	Offices
Osborne House, IoW	English Heritage
Osmaston Manor, Derbys	Demolished 1964
Osterley Park, London	National Trust
Overstrand Hall, Norfolk	Activity centre
Owlpen Manor, Glos	Privately owned, Sir Nicholas and Lady Mander

P

Padworth House, Berks	School
Painshill Park, Surrey	Elmbridge Borough Council (Painshill House was divided into separate properties and sold off in 1948)
Pakenham Hall, Co. Westmeath	Seat of the Pakenhams
Pastures, The, Rut	Ownership at present unknown
Patshull Hall, Staffs	Private ownership, conference and wedding venue
Paxton House, Borders	Paxton House Historic Building Preservation Trust
Peckforton Castle, Ches	Hotel
Peckover House, Cambs	National Trust
Pell Wall Hall, Salop	Private ownership, gutted by fire 1986, now being restored
Penrhyn Castle, Gwynedd	National Trust
Penshurst Place, Kent	Viscount De l'Isle
Peper Harow House, Surrey	Nine residential apartments
Perrycroft, Herefs	Ownership at present unknown
Petersham House, Surrey	Ownership at present unknown
Petworth House, Sussex	National Trust
Philipps House, Wilts	National Trust
Pitmedden House, Aberdeenshire	National Trust for Scotland

Pitzhanger Manor, London	Borough of Ealing, now a gallery and museum
Pleasaunce, The, Norfolk	Christian holiday and conference centre
Powis Castle, Powys	National Trust
Preen Manor, Salop	Demolished 1920
Prestwold Hall, Leics	Edward and Juliet Packe-Drury-Lowe
Prior Park, Som	School
Purbrook House, Hants	Demolished 1837
Pusey House, Berks	Privately owned, not open to the public

Q

Quarters, The, Essex	Ownership at present unknown
Queen's House, London	Part of the National Maritime Museum

R

Raby Castle, Durham	Privately owned
Radway Grange, Warwicks	Privately owned
Ragley Hall, Warwicks	Marquess of Hertford, weddings, corporate functions, outdoor events
Raynham Hall, Norfolk	Marquess Townshend
Red House, Kent	National Trust
Revesby Abbey, Lincs	Privately owned
Rodmarton Manor, Glos	Ownership at present unknown
Roehampton House, Surrey	Apartments
Rousham House, Oxon	Privately owned, viewing by prior appointment
Royal Pavilion, Sussex	Brighton and Hove City Council
Rufford Abbey, Notts	English Heritage
Rufford Old Hall, Lancs	National Trust
Ryston Hall, Norfolk	Ownership at present unknown

S

Saltram, Devon	National Trust
Salutation, The, Kent	Privately owned, hotel accommodation
Sandbeck Park, S. Yorks	Earl of Scarbrough
Scampston Hall, N. Yorks	Privately owned
Scarisbrick Hall, Lancs	Scarisbrick Hall Group, school
Scotney Castle, Kent	National Trust
Seaton Delaval Hall, Northumb	National Trust
Sewardstone Manor House, Essex	Ownership at present unknown
Shadwell Park, Norfolk	Privately owned
Shardeloes, Bucks	Private apartments

Sharpham House, Devon	Sustainable living centre
Shelton Abbey, Co. Wicklow	Prison
Sherborne House, Dorset	Ownership at present unknown, undergoing restoration (2010)
Sheringham Hall, Norfolk	National Trust
Shernfold Park, Sussex	Apartments
Shrubland Park, Suffolk	Ownership at present unknown
Shugborough Hall, Staffs	National Trust
Sissinghurst Castle, Kent	National Trust
Slingsby Castle, N. Yorks	Left unfinished, about 1645
Smallwood Manor, Staffs	School with rentable accommodation
Smeaton Manor, W. Yorks	Ownership at present unknown
Snowshill Manor, Glos	National Trust
Somerhill, Kent	Home to three schools
Southill Park, Beds	Privately owned, home of the Whitbreads, not open to the public
St Alban's Court, Kent	The Bruderhof, a Christian religious community
St Edmund's Hill, Suffolk	Now Moreton Hall, a school
St Giles House, Dorset	Earl of Shaftesbury
Standen, Sussex	National Trust
Stanford Hall, Leics	Privately owned
Stanmer House, Sussex	Wedding and conference venue
Stanmore Hall, Salop	Privately owned, apartments
Stanton Harcourt Manor, Oxon	Seat of the Harcourts
Stirling Palace, Stirling	Tourist attraction managed by Historic Scotland
Stobs Castle, Borders	Ownership at present unknown
Stokesay Court, Salop	Privately owned, visiting by prior appointment
Stoneleigh Abbey, Warwicks	'A charitable trust' (unnamed) Parts contain private gathering
Stourhead House, Wilts	National Trust
Stowe House, Bucks	School
Stratfield Saye, Hants	The Duke of Wellington
Studley Royal House, N. Yorks	Destroyed by fire 1946
Sudbrooke House, Surrey	Clubhouse of Richmond Golf Club
Sudbury Hall, Derbys	National Trust
Sutton Scarsdale Hall, Derbys	Ruined, asset-stripped 1919–20
Swallowfield Park, Berks	Apartments
Swinton Park, N. Yorks	Hotel
Syon House, London	Duke of Northumberland

T

Tabley House, Ches	University of Manchester
Tatton Park, Ches	National Trust
Temple Newsam House, W. Yorks	Leeds City Council
Thirlestane Castle, Borders	Thirlestane Castle Trust
Thirsk Hall, N. Yorks	Privately owned
Thoresby Hall, Notts	Spa hotel (Warners former Dukery home)
Thorndon Hall, Essex	Apartments
Thornhill Park, Dorset	Ownership at present unknown
Tigbourne Court, Surrey	Ownership at present unknown
Towneley Hall, Lancs	Burnley Council, museum and art gallery
Treberfydd, Powys	Privately owned, seat of the Raikes family
Tregenna Castle, Cornwall	Hotel
Trentham Hall, Staffs	Demolished 1905 {formerly Dukes of Sutherland of the Leveson-Gower family - wonderful gardens open}
Trerice, Cornwall	National Trust
Tullynally Castle, Co. Westmeath	See Pakenham Hall
Tyntesfield, Som	National Trust
Tyringham Hall, Bucks	Privately owned

U

Umberslade Hall, Warwicks	Apartments
Uppark, Sussex	National Trust

V

Vanbrugh Castle, London	Maisonettes
Vyne, The, Hants	National Trust

W

Waddesdon Manor, Bucks	National Trust
Walcot Hall, Salop	Privately owned, wedding venue
Wallington Hall, Northumb	National Trust
Wanstead House, Essex	Demolished 1820
Wardour Castle, Wilts	See New Wardour Castle
Wasing House, Berks	Destroyed by fire, 1945, stables survive
Wedderburn Castle, Borders	Privately owned, weddings and corporate events
Welbeck Abbey, Notts	Duke of Portland {Army HQ}
Wentworth Castle, S. Yorks	Wentworth Castle and Stainborough Park Heritage Trust

Wentworth Woodhouse, W. Yorks	Privately owned
Westbury Court Garden, Glos	National Trust, house demolished
Weston Park, Staffs	The Weston Park Foundation, tourist attraction
Westonbirt House, Glos	School
Wightwick Manor, W. Mid	National Trust
Wilburton Manor House, Cambs	School
Wildernesse, Kent	See Dorton House
Willey Hall, Salop	Privately owned by Lord Forester, not open to the public
Willington Stables, Beds	National Trust
Wilton Castle, N. Yorks	Apartments
Wilton House, Wilts	Earl of Pembroke
Wilton Park, Bucks	Demolished 1968
Wimpole Hall, Cambs	National Trust
Windsor Castle, Berks	Royal palace
Windy Hill, Renfrewshire	Ownership at present unknown
Witley Court, Worcs	Present ownership unknown, managed by English Heritage. Partially destroyed by fire and asset-stripped, 1937
Wivenhoe Park, Essex	Part of the University of Essex
Woburn Abbey, Beds	Duke of Bedford
Wollaton Hall, Notts	Nottingham City Council, now a museum
Woolton Hall, Lancs	Ownership at present unknown
Worksop Manor, Notts	Privately owned, largely demolished
Wotton House, Bucks	Privately owned
Wrest Park, Beds	English Heritage
Wycombe Abbey, Bucks	School

Y

Yester House, East Lothian	Ownership at present unknown, for sale September 2010

SELECT BIBIOGRAPHY

GENERAL WORKS

Life in the English Country House: a social and architectural history, Mark Girouard (Harmondsworth: Penguin Books, 1980).
The Country House explained, Trevor Yorke (Newbury: Countryside, 2003).
Life in the Country House: a historical dictionary, David N. Durant (London: John Murray, 1996).
How to read a Country House, Jeremy Musson (London: Ebury, 2005).
Country Houses of England, Geoffrey Tyack and Steven Brindle (London: A & C Black, 1994).

ARCHITECTURE AND CONSTRUCTION

A Dictionary of Architecture and Landscape Architecture, James Stevens Curl (2nd ed., Oxford: Oxford University Press, 2006).
England's Thousand Best Houses, Simon Jenkins, with photographs by Quintin Wright (London: Allen Lane, 2003).
Rice's Architectural Primer, Matthew Rice (London: Bloomsbury, 2009)
British Architects and Craftsmen, Sacheverell Sitwell, (London & Malvern Wells: B. T. Batsford, 1945–6).
Clean and Decent: the fascinating history of the bathroom and WC, Lawrence Wright (London: Penguin, 2000).
A Biographical Dictionary of British Architects, 1600–1840, Howard Colvin (4th ed., New Haven & London: Yale University Press, 2008).
The Victorian Country House, Mark Girouard (New Haven & London: Yale University Press, 1979).

INTERIORS AND FURNISHINGS

The National Trust Book of the English House Interior, Geoffrey Beard (London: Penguin in association with the National Trust, 1991).

Craftsmen and Interior Decoration in England, 1660–1820, Geoffrey Beard, (London: Bloomsbury Books, 1986).

Historic Interiors: a photographic tour, photographs by Andreas von Einsiedel and Nadia Mackenzie; text by Margaret Willes (London: National Trust, 1999).

GROUNDS AND GARDENS

Country House Estates, Margaret Willes (London: National Trust, 1996).

Traditional English Gardens, Arabella Lennox-Boyd (Weidenfeld & Nicholson, 1988).

Follies and Pleasure Pavilions, George Mott and Sally Sample Aall (London: Pavilion, 1989).

The Country House Garden: a grand tour, Gervase Jackson-Stops and James Pipkin(London: Pavilion, 1995).

LEISURE AND ENTERTAINMENT

Carriage Terminology: an historical dictionary, Don H. Berkebile (Washington: Smithsonian Institution Press, 1978).

Country House Pastimes, Oliver Garnett (London: National Trust, 1998).

BUILDINGS INDEX

F

G

H

The decline of the Country House & its occupants
see 'The Country House Explored' Trevor Yorke

1894 death duties on agricultural land

By 1883 more than half the acreage of England was owned
by just 4,217 people.
"Why should 10,000 people own 4/5 of England and Wales
so that we become the paupers in our own country" — Lloyd
George

...hated the Lords + nobles, likening the House of Lords to
the unemployed (ie idle & indolent as was the view of the
unemployed at the time)

1909 budget Lloyd George (in Herbert Asquiths government Liberal
1908-16 [Coalition 1915-16]) as Chancellor of the Exchequer
introduced supertaxes, and higher rates of income tax and
hugely increased death duties. George became PM in 1916 with
Asquiths resignation over War reverses.

The great supporter of the peerage Robert Arthur Talbot
Gascoyne-Cecil 3rd marquess of Salisbury and three times
prime minister b 1830 had died in 1903.

The 1908 Liberal policy tried to show the Lords (+ nobles)
as fat, indolent & stupid. Lloyd George hated the sons of
the wealthy who had merely inherited riches & were often
lazy & useless - just having a good time. He stated no
dislike of the wealthy who, had become so, by their own
efforts.

1911 Parliament Act saw the power of veto of the House of
Lords ended so the Liberal Govt was able to introduce
such things as national insurance, health and unemployment
insurances (old age pensions had come in 1908 after the election)
These were all things previously opposed by the Lords who
did not wish to raise the poor above the level of the
observance & workhouse culture where the wealthy preferred
keep them. From this period the poor came to be regarded
as often victims of circumstance and not all idle
layabouts

on landlords "The landlord is no more necessary to agriculture
than a gold chain to a watch."

WWI sounded the death knell of many Country Houses
estates due to many deaths of young sons with no inheritors
left. Plus greatly increased wages after the manpower losses
the war thus increasing hugely the costs of running a
large household. Also came greatly increased costs for fighting
...thing & maintaining many of the large houses causing some
...owning families to live in just a small section of the place.
...nother problem was that few ordinary workers wanted a life
service when they could get better wages & greater independence
industry.

Lightning Source UK Ltd.
Milton Keynes UK
UKOW050457051112

201672UK00005B/5/P